CONTENTS

SEEKING THE TRUTH OF THINGS

confessions of a (catholic) philosopher

∽

Al Gini

Thank you for these kind words and so much more!

Al Gini

9/54/10

acta
PUBLICATIONS

SEEKING THE TRUTH OF THINGS
confessions of a (catholic) philosopher
by Al Gini

Edited by Gregory F. Augustine Pierce
Cover by Tom A. Wright
Text design and typesetting by Patricia A. Lynch

Copyright © 2010 Al Gini

Published by ACTA Publications, 4848 N. Clark Street, Chicago, IL 60640, (800) 397-2282, www.actapublications.com

Library of Congress Catalog number: 2010932999
ISBN: 978-0-87946-43108
Printed in the United States of America by Versa Press
Year 20 19 18 17 16 15 14 13 12 11 10
Printing 15 14 13 12 11 10 9 8 7 6 5 4 3 2 First

To my grandchildren, Tyler and Siena, much love!

Nonno dei Libri

FOREWORD

Al Gini, our professor of business ethics here at Loyola University Chicago, asked me to write a few words of introduction to *Seeking the Truth of Things: confessions of a (catholic) philosopher.*

A metaphor comes to mind, probably because Dr. Gini and I share most Italians' fondness for good food.

A true "public intellectual" is like a great chef. He or she must serve up the truth with imagination and variety, with bits of wisdom served up in doses we can manage, in flavors that entice, enough to satisfy without overwhelming. Both as a nation and as citizens of an ever-expanding and interdependent world, we all have more than a few things on our plate. Who will help us digest it all? Dr. Gini uses his personal story—falling in love with the search for wisdom from his college days onward—to entice us to the table of philosophy and to enthrall us there.

Since I had the same exposure to "the classics" as Dr. Gini, it is delightful to be reminded of their continued relevance. For those who have not had access to such a philosophical education, Gini's reflections are a great place to start. Like Plato, he insists we start with ourselves. In this, the reader has both model and guide in these pages. What better advice than to question ourselves, our prejudices, and presuppositions?

So, who am I? What do I owe others? What ought I to do with my life and my "too many" choices?

These are the age-old and ever urgent questions faced by each of us, the plight and the privilege of every human being. The reader will enjoy feasting at the table of this rare and gifted public intellectual.

Also, Al Gini is a very funny man.

Michael J. Garanzini, S.J., PhD
President of Loyola University Chicago

PROLOGUE

**The study of philosophy
is not that we may know what [others] have thought,
but what the truth of things is.**

Thomas Aquinas

Halfway through my senior year in college, I told my parents that I was not going to apply to law school or medical school or even pursue an advanced degree in history. They were horrified: "What will you do?" they cried out, almost in unison. "I've applied for a PhD program in philosophy," I said proudly, if also a little defensively. My mother stared at me blankly, seemingly struck dumb by my response. My father, on the other hand, was both furious and insulted by my decision.

"You've got to be kidding me!" he yelled. "After getting great grades and setting yourself up for a real career, you're going to throw it away on a frou-frou degree in philosophy?"

"You're joking, right?" Dad continued. "What the hell are you going to do? Sit under a tree with a group of your hippie friends, talking stupid stuff like how many angels can dance on the head of a pin?"

"Dad," I started to say.

"Don't 'dad' me!" he shouted. "And by the way, the answer is seven. Seven angels can dance on a pin at once...or maybe eight, if two of them are anorexic!"

We all laughed at his unexpected and improvised joke, but the rest of the conversation was anything but funny. My mother and father reminded me that sooner or later I'd have to get a job. They suggested that if I loved philosophy I should read it at night or on my vacations. They told me how

9

much they had hoped I would go to law school.

"Law school," Dad said, "being a lawyer. Now that's real work, important work, and you'll make great money! Please son, don't be a *testa duro*" (Italian for "hard head").

"This philosophy stuff…FUGIDDABOUTIT!" (Honest, that's what Dad said, forty-five years before *The Sopranos*.)

As in Willie Nelson's soulful song, "Mamas, don't let your babies grow up to be cowboys," my parents definitely did not want me to grow up to be a philosopher. Looking back all these years later, however, I never regretted my decision. Although my dad was right about one thing: Lawyers do make a lot more money than philosophers.

Then there was this other problem. I was a Roman Catholic. From the cradle. From the old country. On both the Gini and Palmeri side. How could a Catholic be a philosopher? We Catholics had all the answers, didn't we? And if we didn't, the pope would tell us what to think anyway. Catholics couldn't possibly make good philosophers, could we? Would I have to leave my faith in order to learn how to think for myself?

For me, however, the word *philosophy* has always described my job—not just my paid employment but also my vocation in life as well as my relationship to Catholicism.

In Latin, the word *philo* (love) + *sophia* (wisdom) means "the love of wisdom." And, by extension, a philosopher is "one who loves wisdom." The medievals referred to the study of philosophy as "the love of wisdom for wisdom's sake alone," or "the pursuit of knowledge for knowledge itself alone." Philosophy is about *sapientia* (Latin), the pursuit of wisdom, values, and meaning, and not about *technologia* (Greek), the acquisition of skills, crafts, and techniques. For the medievals, philosophy was part of the *artes liberales*, the liberal arts, those studies that liberated or freed a person's mind and heart—not merely satisfied his or her material and bodily needs and requirements.

The ultimate Catholic philosopher, Thomas Aquinas, was, I think, correct when he pointed out that the study of philosophy is about ideas and the true function of ideas, not simply about discovering what other people might have thought or said at different points in history. Thus, the business of philosophy is not the communication and perpetuation of a particular creed or system but rather communicating and instilling a general attitude toward life, one which is open and observant and grounded in the habit of critical inquiry and reflective curiosity. As a philosophy teacher, I have always thought my primary task is to expose my students to ideas—both new and old—and to challenge them to examine the impact these ideas might have on their lives, as individuals and as members of the human race.

I believe ideas matter and move us, and the goal of philosophy is to be better able to understand, cope with, and manage these ideas in both our private and collective lives.

Over the past forty years or so, I've tried to challenge my students—in a Jesuit Catholic University, no less—to be "respectfully disrespectful" of the ideas of others. I've encouraged them to dissect and debate conventional wisdom of all kinds. I've asked them to focus on the abstract and the ethereal as well as on the obvious and the obtuse. I've urged them to make up their own minds. I've tried to steer them toward the perennial questions: What is the meaning of life, death, God, integrity, honor, ethics? But I've always stopped short of suggesting that there are any perennial or absolute answers. There may be such answers, but I don't push them because I don't know them.

I don't advocate pure skepticism. But I do want my students to decide things for themselves, not simply to regurgitate what they've been told, be it by professor, parent, priest, pope, or pundit. In the words of John Stuart Mill, beliefs that are not tested by personal reflection, rational criticism, and fearless discussion tend to be held as "dead dogma and not living truth."[1]

I actually think this questioning approach to philosophy is exactly what the Catholic Church needs and—at its best—wants. The word *catholic*, in fact, means "universal" or "for everyone." That is why I call myself a "catholic" philosopher with a lowercase "c," because I want to be open to understanding and appreciating all philosophies—not just defending one. For me, being a catholic thinker means being a thoughtful person in the world: a person who reflects on his or her rights and obligations in regard to others; a person who feels compelled and concerned about issues that transcend the simplistic equation of "me, myself, and I"; a person who tries to understand that, although all human beings are unique individuals, we are communal creatures in need of one another.

Over the years, my role as teacher has expanded beyond the confines of the classroom. Due in large measure to luck, timing, and circumstance, I've been somewhat sought after as a public speaker as well as a corporate presenter and consultant. For over twenty years, I have also been a regular contributor on the National Public Radio station in Chicago, *Chicago Public Radio* (WBEZ – 91.5 FM), where I've done over six-hundred shows. My official title at the station is "Resident Philosopher," and in my segments I try to cover some philosophical or ethical issue in the news or a general topic I think is worth bringing to my audiences' attention.

What I've tried to do on these shows and with these topics is essentially the same thing I do in the classroom: I serve as a translator. That is, I define, describe, and take the topic apart. I raise issues, ask questions, offer some alternatives, and invite the listening audience to decide for themselves. Yes, I also offer my opinions. I wouldn't be my parents' son if I didn't. In fact, I sometimes editorialize at length on questions or topics I feel passionate about. But I try to never say that mine is the only, or even the best, possible answer available. What I want to do is to provoke thought and be a catalyst for moral reasoning. I want to challenge my students and my audiences to examine their values and beliefs on a topic and then decide for themselves what's right, just, and true.

Because I think that philosophy is best served and taught when it is regarded as a method of inquiry or habit of critical reflection, I have not studied or taught philosophy in a systematic or historically-based way. I have, rather, been drawn to individual topics, issues, and questions such as meaning, sin, choice, moral courage, work, even the importance of laughter and leisure in our lives. In some sense, I suppose, I am a dilettante in the old-fashioned meaning of the term. *Dilettante* comes from the Latin (*dilectore*) and the Italian (*dilettare*), which mean "to delight," "to admire," and, by extension, "a person who loves the arts." A true dilettante, therefore, is a person who cultivates a love for a particular topic and pursues it passionately.

It is unfortunate that we now generally use the term to suggest that a dilettante is an amateur, someone who has a superficial interest in a topic, a person who dabbles in something without serious study or commitment. (Ironically enough, this approach to philosophy would have been *exactly* what my father would have preferred for me: make a lot of money as a lawyer and then be a dilettante about philosophy in my spare time.)

Like most people, I am left somewhat cold and overwhelmed by Kant's *Critique of Pure Reason*, Wittgenstein's *Tractatus Logico-Philosophicus*, or Russell's and Whitehead's *Principia Mathematica*. But just because I am not drawn to the levels of abstraction involved in metaphysics, epistemology, and meta-mathematical analysis, it does not mean that I am not a dedicated student in passionate pursuit of Socrates' philosophical challenge to us all: to escape doing wrong and to live well with others.

This book is about some of the lessons I've learned while attending the University of Life. It's about some of the issues and ideas I am both personally and professionally passionate about. The methodology I use in pursuing these topics is both time-honored and elegantly simple. As James Rachels succinctly put it: "Philosophy…is first and last an exercise in reason…. The ideas that should come out on top are the ones that have the best reason on their side."[2] This, for me, is what it means to be a catholic philosopher. I think Thomas Aquinas himself would agree with me.

I

HOW I FELL IN LOVE WITH PHILOSOPHY

Know thyself.

Socrates

In days of old, when knights were bold, and dragons still roamed the earth, I went off to college. I was only the second person in my family to graduate from high school and the first to attend college. Because I had no idea what I wanted to major in or do with my life, my academic advisor wisely suggested that I get the basic core requirements out of the way and worry about declaring a major after I had a few semesters under my belt. While going over the class options for my first semester in school, I came across Philosophy 101, and immediately registered for it. I thought it was a perfect choice: It fulfilled a requirement; it fit into my schedule; and, in my naïveté, I mistakenly thought I was signing up for Psychology 101. I figured that the class would be all about sex. Boy, was I wrong. And in retrospect, how lucky for me that I was.

On the first day of philosophy class, the professor walked in and, without a hello or a nod to any of us, marched to the front of the room. His hair and tie were completely askew, and, even though it was a very hot September day, he was wearing a wool tweed sport jacket, corduroy trousers, and a scruffy pair of thick-soled wing tip shoes. After depositing his stack of books and papers on the podium, he took out a Zippo lighter, a pack of imported French non-filtered *Gauloises* cigarettes, and lit up. (Remember, this was the early 1960s.)

The professor smoked and stared out at us without saying a word for what, at the time, seemed interminable. He inhaled his cigarette with a fe-rocity and intensity I had never witnessed before. My father smoked, but not like this man. At some very basic level that I was unable to understand at the time, my professor seemed to be totally involved in the act of smok-ing. To him, smoking seemed to be more of a passionate desire rather than a mere addiction. It was as if smoking was some form of religious ritual. He seemed to consume the smoke, absorbing it into his system, converting it into some weird sort of energy or fuel. It was as if he was using the smoke as a catalyst for his thinking. (I would come to find out that my first professor wasn't the only philosopher that smoked. In the 1960s and 1970s, smoking was part and parcel of playing the role of being an intellectual—or as they then preferred to be called—the *cognoscente*. There seemed to be a direct correlation between philosophical disputation, coffeehouses, and smoking. Full disclosure requires me to confess, that I too fell vulnerable to the smok-ing mystique and puffed away for over twenty-five years. *Mea culpa*. Being a catholic, however, I know that I have been forgiven already.)

After finishing an entire cigarette and speed inhaling half of another, the professor suddenly began to speak to us in a calm and pleasant manner. "This class is officially listed as 'Introduction to Philosophy,'" he said. "And as titles go, it's accurate. That's exactly what I'm going to try to do this semes-ter—introduce you to philosophy.

"But, I'm not going to do it by making you read bits and pieces of all the major Western philosophers over the last twenty-five hundred years. That would make this class a history course, which it's not. The history of and the doing of philosophy are different things. Philosophy cannot be taught in the same way as geography or astronomy, because it is not primarily con-cerned with knowledge of specific facts. Rather, he said, "it's concerned with knowledge as reflection, knowledge as criticism, and knowledge as value awareness. Such concerns cannot be easily codified into a list of theorems or truisms, or by reciting all the basic facts and dates of all the major philo-sophical theories."

He paused, lit yet another cigarette, and then said to us, almost in a lover's whisper, "Philosophy is about *sapientia*: the pursuit of wisdom, values, meaning, and a careful examination of the purpose of life. To do this, we don't need to read history, we just need to read Socrates and try to figure out for ourselves what he meant when he suggested that the goal of life is not to escape death, suffering, or inconvenience. The goal of life is to escape doing wrong and to live well with others."

With that, the professor tamped out his cigarette, handed out a stack of syllabi, said that we should read *The Apology* for our next class meeting, and walked out without saying another word. Some of the students were stunned by his unusual performance. Others were confused or intimidated by it. I was fascinated and hooked for life.

The English philosopher and mathematician Alfred North Whitehead once said that "all philosophy is but a footnote to Socrates/Plato." Plato, of course, was a student of Socrates for 20 years and served as the chronicler and creator of the Socratic dialogues. What Whitehead meant by this statement is that Socrates and Plato laid the groundwork for what Western philosophy was to become. Certainly, they were not the first philosophers; they were preceded by Thales, Anaximander, Pythagoras, Heraclitus, Parmenides, Zeno, and others. However, Socrates and Plato were the first "students of wisdom" who left behind a set of writings, and within this body of work we can find most if not all of the basic philosophical questions asked, even if they were not satisfactorily answered or resolved. It has been argued, by better minds than me, that after Socrates and Plato, the rest of the history of philosophy has been an attempt to unpack, embellish, and formulate answers to the questions, topics, and problems they raised.

Students of classical Greek history have long debated exactly where Socrates' thoughts and ideas left off and where Plato's began. Though there is no unanimity on the matter, most scholars agree that the dialogue *The Apology* is a reflection of Socrates' most fundamental philosophical beliefs.

In *The Apology*, Socrates argues that the first principle and the first job of philosophy is to be able to grasp and understand the admonition of the oracle of Apollo at Delphi: *Gnothi seuton*, "Know thyself."

Socrates was "curiously unscientific" about his outlook on life.[1] He said of himself that he had "nothing to do with physical speculations." Nor was he especially interested in one of Aristotle's primary preoccupations, metaphysics, which is the study of the ultimate cause(s), purpose(s), and meaning(s) of life. Rather than questioning the nature and structure of the cosmos, Socrates believed we would be better off questioning the cosmos within—our inner nature, our most intimate selves. For him, the first question of philosophy is the self: Who am I? To answer the question, Socrates believed we must ask questions that disturb, provoke, anger, challenge, and confront us. We must be willing to ask questions that shake and shift the ground under our feet.[2] For Socrates, the question of self (Who am I?) precedes all other considerations, including the related question of self and others (What ought I to do with others?). As Socrates clearly stated in *The Republic*, "He who would rule the world must first rule himself."

In *The Apology*, Socrates argues that the first step toward wisdom is the discovery and acknowledgement of our own ignorance. He tells the story of his friend Chaerephon, who climbed up the slopes of Mount Parnassus and asked the oracle if there was a wiser man in all of Greece than Socrates of Athens. The priestess replied that there was no one wiser, and Socrates was shocked by the oracle's answer. "What can the god mean?" said Socrates. "I have no claim to wisdom, great or small." So Socrates decided this was a test, and he set out to find the wisest man in all of Greece. He talked to politicians, poets, skilled craftsmen, and many others thought to be wise. But although they all appeared or claimed to be wise, they were not. Moreover, Socrates said, even when they obviously did not know something, they denied their ignorance and asserted their wisdom. In the end, Socrates decided that the oracle was correct: He was the wisest man in all of Greece. Or at least he was wise to this small extent: "I do not claim to know what I do not know." It is also in *The Apology* that Socrates declares, for all Athenians to hear:

I spent all my time going about trying to persuade you, young and old, to make your first and your chief concern not for your bodies or your possession, but for the highest welfare of your souls…. Wealth does not bring goodness, but goodness brings wealth and every other blessing, both to the individual and to the state…. Let no day pass without discussing goodness…. [This] is really the very best thing that a [person] can do, and…life without this sort of examination is not worth living. [3]

For Socrates and his modern successors in the "study of the mind," the discipline we now call *psychology*, including Abraham Maslow and Sigmund Freud—the "examined life" is the result of self-awareness, self-reflection, and ultimately self-knowledge. It is only in coming to know ourselves, both our strengths and weaknesses, that we can begin to have sympathy, care, and concern for others. As Maslow so elegantly phrased it, "What we are blind and deaf to in ourselves, we are blind and deaf to in others." For Socrates, the art of living together in the *polis* (the city-state) and the science of human behavior and conduct start with self, but they are lived out with others. For Socrates, the good life for self and the good life with others (an ethical life) are the same. Both constitute a life lived "according to what is reasonable" (*kata ton orthon logos*).

Many scholars believe that one of the central features of the Socratic dialogues is their lack of doctrinaire ideology. Socrates did not preach "a system." Rather Socrates was a teacher, and what he taught was not so much a full-blown, comprehensive philosophy as it was a way of looking at the world and of looking at self. The essence of his lesson plan was an elegant one: Let us all talk and reason together. For him, philosophy was a communal event, not a singular activity. Truth, as a way to achieve good behavior, is the result of thinking with and talking to others. It is the end product of dialogue. Thus we call it this kind of dialogue the "Socratic" or the "dialectical" method.

This method requires us to enter into conversation with others in order to examine or debate an idea or a subject matter. Theoretically, the dialogue proceeds from a less adequate definition, or from a consideration of particular examples, to a more general definition. (Metaphorically speaking, the dialectical method is the practice of holding a problem out at arm's length to better see it and gain a modicum of objectivity. In so examining the problem, alternative solutions are applied until the best possible one is hit upon.) Socratic scholar Gregory Vlastos described Socrates' method of inquiry as "among the greatest achievements of humanity." Why? Because, says Vlastos, it makes philosophical inquiry "a common human enterprise, open to every [person]." Instead of requiring allegiance to a specific philosophical viewpoint or analytical technique or specialized vocabulary, the Socratic method "calls for common sense and common speech." And this, says Vlastos, "is as it should be, for how a [person] should live is [everyone's] business." [4]

Christopher Phillips, author of the charming and insightful *Socrates Café*, argues that the Socratic method goes far beyond Vlastos' description. The method, says Phillips, does not merely call for common sense in our lives, but it also examines and critiques what common sense actually is in our lives. The method asks: Does the common sense (conventional wisdom) of our day offer us the greatest potential for self-understanding and ethical conduct? Or is the prevailing common sense in fact a roadblock to realizing this potential? According to Phillips, the Socratic method forces people to confront their own dogmatism by asking basic questions such as: What does this mean? What speaks for and against it? Are there other ways of considering the issue that are even more plausible and tenable? In compelling us to explore alternative perspectives, says Phillips, the method forces us to think outside the box and be open to the opinions of others. [5]

For Socrates, we are "questioning beings," and it is only through questioning life and others that we begin to have a better understanding of self. In fact, he suggests that the process of questioning is more important than the answers arrived at. When Socrates said, "The unexamined life is not worth living," what is implied is that even if we question life we still may not come up with an answer, much less the right answer. Or we may simply generate a series of new questions. Or, worse yet, we might arrive at an answer that we cannot or will not accept. Nevertheless, Socrates seemed convinced that the greatest error, the biggest danger, lies with not asking any questions at all. In asking questions, we say and assert something about ourselves. In asking, we have hope, but we also recognize that there are no guarantees. And, in asking, we reveal a great deal about who we are and who we would like to be.

In *The Apology*, with his very life in the balance, Socrates retains his conviction that the greatest danger of all is to dispense with the questioning and examining of our lives:

> *As long as I breathe and have the strength to go on, I won't quit philosophizing. I won't quit exhorting you and whomever I happen to meet, in my customary way. Esteemed friend, citizen of Athens, the greatest city in the world, so outstanding in both intelligence and power, aren't you ashamed to care so much to make all the money you can, and to advance your reputation and prestige—while for truth and wisdom and the improvement of your soul you have no care or worry?* [6]

For Socrates, philosophy was a way of life, a way of approaching and seeing the world, a way of thinking. Philosophy is something we live out with others. And in this "living out" we are constantly asking ourselves three fundamental questions: Who am I; what do I owe others; what ought I do? In the end, the Socratic method is as much about the process as the product, as much about the journey as the destination. In fact, I think it is fair to say that what Socrates left us was not a series of answers but a series of questions and a purposeful way of thinking. In the words of Ludwig W. Wittgenstein, "Philosophy is not a theory but an activity."

If I had to put this all together so I could come up with a nicely gift-wrapped conclusion, it would sound something like this. Philosophy is a way of looking at the world. It is a method that is more concerned with teaching people *how to* rather than *what to* think. If I'm right in this, philosophy more closely resembles an unending search than it does the acquisition of a fixed prize or singular answer. To put it yet another way, the Socratic tradition does not require that we all reason alike, but rather that we all reason together.

What could be more catholic (with a small "c") than that?

II

THE EXAMINED LIFE

We are all philosophers because our condition demands it. We live every moment in a universe of seemingly eternal thoughts and ideas, yet simultaneously in the constantly churning and decaying world of our bodies and their humble situations. The result is a nagging need to find meaning.

Russell Shorto

Although philosophy and the study of philosophy have a long history, it has not always been an honored one. In fact, philosophers and philosophy have been regularly subjected to ridicule and scorn. Ambrose Bierce, the nineteenth century American author and critic, once defined philosophy as "a route of many roads, leading from nowhere to nothing."[1] Fellow American, William James, sadly lamented that far too many people uncritically believed that a philosopher was "a blind man in a dark room looking for a black hat that is not there."[2] More contemporaneously, psychologist Robert R. Provine denigrates philosophy as being neither scientific nor completely logical in its methodology and conclusions. "Philosophy," he says, "is to science, what alcohol is to sex: It may stir the imagination, fire the passions, and get the process underway, but the act and implementation may be flawed, and the end result may come up short." Provine believes that many philosophers fail because they have "an overly optimistic estimate of the power of naked reason and dependence on anecdotal evidence."[3] I think that all of these characterizations are incorrect.

Philosophy is part of the process by which we try to participate in the University of Life. Philosophy is an attempt to understand and make sense out of the ideas, feelings, facts, and lifestyles we live by and live with. For me, philosophy begins, as Aristotle suggested, in wonder and curiosity. Or, it grows out of the fear of our own ignorance. Although the Danish philosopher Sören Kierkegaard can be a bit overly dramatic, perhaps his personal reflections and lamentations best exemplify the beginning of philosophical thinking.

> *One sticks one's finger into the soil to tell by the smell in what land one is: I stick my finger into existence—it smells of nothing. Where am I? Who am I? How came I here? What is this thing called the world? What does this world mean? Who is it that has lured me into this thing and now leaves me there? How did I come into the world? Why was I not consulted…but was thrust into the ranks as though I had been bought of a kidnapper, a dealer in souls? How did I obtain an interest in this big enterprise they call reality? Why should I have an interest in it? Is it not a voluntary concern? And if I am compelled to take part in it, where is the director…where shall I turn with my complaint?[4]*

Allow me to also offer you Blaise Pascal's stylish French musings on the wondrous mystery of existence itself:

> *When I consider the short duration of my life, swallowed up in the eternity before and after, the little space which I fill, and even can see, engulfed in the infinite immensity of space of which I am ignorant, and which knows me not, I am frightened and I am astonished at being here rather than there and why now rather than then?[5]*

Philosophy, like the process of education itself, is about critical reflection and analysis. To be reflective, to be critical, does not mean to simply find fault, rip apart, or deny. To be reflective means to carefully examine, to ask all kinds of questions—including those questions that intimidate us and make us want to stop thinking about them. The purpose of philosophy is to turn us upside-down and rotate us on an axis in order to see the world from a different perspective.

Cultural critic Theodore Roszak claims that philosophy is "the process of questioning the foundations of relevance." Or as Alfred North Whitehead ironically put it, "Philosophy asks the simple question, 'What is it (life) all about?'" In other words, the essence of philosophy is its willingness to ask uncomfortable questions about everything. It asks questions that we take for granted. Questions that are obvious and basic, but the answers to which are so fundamental that without some kind of answer life would be unbearable and rudderless. Questions as immediate and as unavoidable as: What is truth? What is death? Who am I? How came I to be? What are my obligations to others?

The pursuit of philosophy is not about creating systems or specific answers. Philosophy is itself a way of life, a method of looking at the world. It is the activity of dissecting, examining, and questioning everything. When Socrates said, "The examined life is not worth living," what he implied was that when we philosophize we make ourselves more responsive to, and responsible for, the life we live. In pursuing the question of self, we come to realize that we are communal creatures; that we are dependent upon one another to survive and thrive; that—like it or not—we are moral creatures. And, as moral creatures, we realize that choices must be made. We call these choices "ethics." The unavoidable fact is that whether our choices are good or bad, our collective existence requires us to continually decide what we ought to do in regard to others and to the universe in which we find ourselves.

In recognizing that we are not the sole center of that universe, we are required to transcend the simplistic equation of "me, myself, and I." We are required to consider the rights of others. We are required to do something we do not always want to do, which is to be our best rational selves. We are required to step outside the shadow of self, and be, as St. Ignatius of Loyola put it, a man or woman for others.

The spirit of the philosophical enterprise is succinctly captured in Albert Einstein's words of advice to young scientists. "Don't be afraid to make mistakes. Don't be afraid to ask silly questions. Don't feel guilty when you don't take the advice of an expert."[6] Philosophy is primarily a method of inquiry, a means of thought by which you approach an issue or a problem. It tries to examine and understand the situation for what it is. Philosophy is not a prearranged bundle of truths—there are no hidden presuppositions. It is an approach, not just an answer.

Perhaps the real profit of a philosophical education is the ability it gives to discriminate, to make distinctions that penetrate below the surface. We may not be able to lay hold of the realities beneath the froth and foam, but at least those of us who are philosophically educated do not take the froth and foam to *be* the realities. We know there is a difference between sound and sense, between what is empathic and what is distinctive, between what is conspicuous and what is important. In the end, philosophy is concerned with teaching people *how* to think, not *what* to think. William James helps to clarify this point when he says: "What doctrines students take from their teachers are of little consequence provided they catch from them the living, philosophical attitude of mind, the independent personal look at all the data of life, and then the eagerness to harmonize (understand) them…."[7]

Whether you are catholic of the "upper" or "lower" case variety, it seems to me that there are a number of writers and thinkers within the Church's tradition that spent their careers living out the essence of exactly what William James meant by the "philosophical attitude of mind." A short list of some of those thinkers who pursued, preached, taught, and wrote about the perennial questions of life and philosophy would include: Augustine of Hippo, Peter Abelard, Hildegard of Bingen, Albert the Great, John Duns Scotus, William of Ockham, Thomas More, Gertrude Elizabeth Margaret Anscombe, G.K. Chesterton, Jacques Maritain, E'tienne-Henry Gilson, Bernard Lonergan, and Eleonore Stump. My personal pantheon of philosophical favorites includes Thomas Aquinas, Teilhard de Chardin, Dorothy Day, and John Paul II. I am both intellectually and emotionally drawn to these very different individuals because each of them, in their own way, dedicated themselves to the pursuit of truth, goodness, beauty, and justice.

Thomas Aquinas plays a pivotal role in the history of philosophical thought. As a teacher, writer, and Doctor of the Church, the central thrust of his enormous body of work was an attempt to find a *modus vivendi* between faith and philosophy. (Of course, Aquinas himself was enormous, weighing over 250 pounds and ironically nicknamed the "Dumb Ox" by Chesterton.) For Aquinas, although philosophy and theology were two different ways of looking at reality, he wanted to show that reason need not be in conflict with faith and that faith can be better understood or clarified by the use of reason. Thomas' attempt was to "defang" the prejudicial proposition that reason was always limited and therefore fallible, and simultaneously "dethrone" the belief that theological truths are impervious to rational debate or analysis.

For Aquinas, reason and faith are the basic tools by which we try to grasp and deal with the perennial questions of life: How came things to be? What is the meaning of life? What do I owe others? What is the nature of God? The answers we come up with to address these questions can be based purely on either reason or faith, but for Aquinas the best possible answers are illuminated by both.

Although trained in philosophy in a Jesuit seminary, Pierre Teilhard de Chardin developed his revolutionary philosophical world view primarily in a laboratory as a geologist and paleontologist. Without our getting bogged down in scientific theory and prolonged debate concerning Chardin's mystical views on the nature of God, for me Chardin's life and work helped to absolve the Church of her sin against Galileo and science. Galileo was silenced and sequestered because his scientifically trained mind and his observations of the heavens, using the crudest of telescopes, disproved the Church's homocentric view of the universe that the sun and the stars rotated around the earth. Even when Galileo begged one of his Cardinal Inquisitors to look up to the heavens with his telescope, his accuser refused to do so. Reportedly, he said to Galileo: "I cannot risk observing with my eyes that which my faith will not allow me to accept with my heart and mind."

In embracing and advocating evolutionary theory and humankind's development in the evolutionary process, Chardin's teachings and writings eventually led the twentieth century Church to accept the fact that God and science need not be opposed. Through the use of logic, observation, and the scientific method, Chardin helped to overthrow the barriers that the Church had erected and steadfastly maintained between the laws of nature and the laws of God. In so doing, Chardin reaffirmed Aquinas' central contention that reason can be compatible with faith.

My last two philosophical role models may not, at first glance, seem to fit the usual descriptions of what we think of as a philosopher. However, if John Dewey was right when he suggested that philosophers are people who, when they see a problem, seek out possible alternatives, decide on a plan, and then act on it—both Dorothy Day and John Paul II are card-carrying members of the club! (And least we forget, in 1953, long before Karol Józef Wojtyla was elected pope, he earned a PhD in philosophy on the ethics of Max Scheler at Lublin Catholic University.)

Dorothy Day was a writer, a revolutionary thinker, a person of ideas and ideals—but primarily she was a person of action. For Day, the problems of life were not to be only lamented, dissected, and studied. Life required energy and involvement. Problems were not paintings or photos simply to be contemplated. Problems required action and resolution. For Day, the achievement of ethics and justice in society required both contemplation and conduct.

Founder and editor of *The Catholic Worker* newspaper, Day's explicit and constant goal was to publicize Catholic social teaching and to promote steps to bring about the peaceful transformation of society. Day's long-term desire was justice and not just charity. When her critics chided her with Jesus' comment that "the poor would always be with us," her reply was both humble and poignantly assertive. "Yes it's true, but we are not content that there should be so many of them. The class structure is of our making and by our consent, not God's, and we must do what we can to change it."[8] Incensed by the unfairness of the capitalistic system, she sought an economy based on human needs, rather than on the profit motive. In pursuit of this end, she lived her life based on the principles of the Sermon on the Mount and dedicated herself to "comforting the afflicted and afflicting the comfortable."

Although I am uncomfortable with some of John Paul II's edicts and pronouncements (for example, his position on the status and importance of women within the Church), I am profoundly moved by his views on the importance of work in our lives, which he articulated in his landmark encyclical, *On Human Work (Laborem Exercens)*. John Paul II argues that from the beginning we are called to work. Work is one of the distinguishing characteristics of humankind. Work preoccupies our existence on earth. Life is built up every day from work, and we are able to either derive a specific kind of dignity from it or suffer both social and economic harm. This is why, warns the pope, individual nations and the international community must always keep in mind that—although we are "destined" to work, "need" to work, indeed, "called" to work—work is for humankind, and not humankind for work.

For John Paul II, work "is the axis of human self-making."[9] Work is how we become "more a human being." In work we make our world and simultaneously actualize and fulfill our potentialities. As pope, what John Paul II meant is that work is the enabling force that allows men and women to act as "divine agents" for the transformation of life on earth. In other words, work becomes the vehicle by which human beings exercise co-creationship in the world and share in the activity of the Creator. As a philosopher and ethicist, what Karol Józef Wojtyla means is that we are co-responsible for our lives. Through work we actualize ourselves, assume responsibility for our own private decisions, and contribute to our communal future. Our work is both a particular reflection of ourselves and a mark of our collective humanity. For Wojtyla "work" is the key to the central ethical question: "How can we make life more human?"

As a "lowercase" catholic, I believe that Catholicism has something to offer the world regarding ethics and values. I believe in the struggle for the Kingdom of God, here and now, on earth. I believe in the Church's positions on social justice and corporate social responsibility. I believe in the Church's teachings on conscience and personal responsibility. And I believe that being a Catholic of any variety doesn't make us worse philosophers than non-Catholics, but it doesn't necessarily make us better ones either. We still need to think clearly, to question assumptions, to create new and better ways of looking at the world, ourselves, and one another. Our goal, like that of all people, is (in the words of Socrates) to "escape doing wrong and live well with others." If our Catholic faith helps us to do this, then we need to use it. If our pursuit of philosophy makes the achievement of that goal easier or more productive, then we need to use that as well.

III

THE NEED FOR MEANING

The reasonable man adapts himself to the world. The unreasonable one persists in trying to adapt the world to himself. Therefore, all progress depends on the unreasonable man.

George Bernard Shaw

Over the years my students, friends, and acquaintances have asked me to name my very favorite philosophy book. For a long time I found the question both intimidating and very difficult to answer. They wanted *one* book, presumably a book that would move and change them; a book that would give them insight and perspective; a book that would offer them a philosophical road map by which they could navigate the confusing and complex geography of life.

Frankly, it was a tall order for a single book, no matter how good I thought it was, and for years I just could not put my finger on one that would even come close to fulfilling their expectations. And so instead, in true academic form, I would give people a long list of books that even a full-time graduate student in philosophy would have found daunting. I recommended Plato's *Republic*, Aristotle's *Nicomachean Ethics*, John Rawl's *A Theory of Justice*, Augustine's *Confessions*, Immanuel Kant's *Foundations of the Metaphysics of Morals*, Martin Heidegger's *Being and Time*, and Thomas Aquinas' *Summa Contra Gentiles*.

As I ticked off my list, I could always see the disappointment in their eyes. They smiled and thanked me. But, not so surprisingly, none of my interlocutors ever got back to me wanting just a few more titles to add to my ponderous and pretentious reading list.

And then one summer, as I was plowing my own way through Alan Bullock's classic analysis of evil, *Hitler: A Study in Tyranny*, I suddenly realized that there is a single book that I have long admired and can unequivocally recommend to those of the just-give-me-one-book-to-get-started ilk. It is Viktor Frankl's *Man's Search for Meaning*.

As a small "c" catholic philosopher, I should have thought of this book much sooner. Frankl was a Jew, and we catholic philosophers are direct philosophical descendents of the Jews. Ever since Job first grappled with the question of bad things happening to good people, we have been infatuated with the basic question: "What's it all about, Alfie?"

Frankl's thesis is easy to state, which is that striving to find meaning in one's life is the primary motivational force in human experience. Without meaning, we have no focus or purpose and lose our foothold on reality and even our desire to "be." Of course, the full import and power of his thesis can only be fully appreciated when you understand where Frankl conceived it and how he lived it out and ultimately proved it.

Viktor Frankl was born in Vienna of parents of Jewish descent in 1905. He completed his MD studies in 1930 and went on to specialize in psychiatry. In September of 1942, Frankl, his father, mother, brother, and new bride were arrested and sent to Auschwitz. Suddenly he found himself stripped of every element of his identity: his family, his profession, his name (he was now number 119,104), the clothes on his back, and, very nearly, his will to survive. Forced to dig ditches twelve hours a day on less than 1,000 calories of food, harassed by brutal guards, waking every morning to the possibility of being "selected" for immediate extermination in the gas chambers, Frankl was forced to confront a number of crucial philosophical questions: *Why is this happening to me? Why must I endure this pain and anguish? Having lost everything, is my life really worth preserving? Can any meaning be found amidst this madness?*

Frankl noted that many of his fellow concentration camp victims could not find the will to go on. The daily horrors, the constant threat of suddenly being beaten or shot for the smallest offense, the continuous feeling of help-lessness and despair led many prisoners to give up and become a "Moslem." A "Moslem," in the hardened and probably racist language of the concentra-tion camps, was a prisoner who stopped shaving, stopped trying, stopped looking fit, dragged himself from task to task, smoked rather than saved his cigarettes, and gave away his extra bread ration. These were the prison-ers who had lost hope and had given up faith in their ability to carry on. These were the ones who could no longer see beyond the moment, or dare to dream, or find any meaning at all in just enduring. "Sooner, or later," said Frankl, "usually sooner, every 'Moslem' goes to the gas chamber."[1]

As a physician, a psychiatrist, and a student of philosophy (he complet-ed his PhD in philosophy in 1948 after the war had ended), Frankl somehow managed to chronicle his own feelings and responses to the living hell of the camps, as well as those of his fellow inmates. For him, the path for survival began with a recognition of just how much he and others had been able to endure. All they had left, said Frankl, was their "naked existence."[2] But they quickly found out two critical things: First, the "[medical] textbooks tell lies!"[3] Human beings are tough enough to endure much more than we think we can, Frankl wrote. If necessary, "a person can get used to anything!"[4]

What this said to Frankl is that the human being is not completely and unavoidably influenced by his or her surroundings. Humankind is not just an accidental by-product of our environmental, biological, psychological, and sociological backgrounds. No matter what our predicament, we do have the ability to transcend our surroundings. We have the ability to make a ba-sic choice.

To be sure, we are finite creatures, and our freedom is restricted. We do not have "freedom *from* the conditions" of life,[5] but we do have the freedom *to* take a stand in regard to the conditions that we face. For Frankl, every-thing can be taken from us except one thing: "The last of the human free-doms—to choose one's attitude in any given set of circumstances, to choose one's own way."[6] Translation: All too often we cannot change or control the facts of life or the course of our fate, but we can control our attitude in regard to the particular facts of fate. He wrote:

> *Even though conditions such as lack of sleep, insufficient food and various mental stresses may suggest that the inmates were bound to react in certain ways, in the final analysis it becomes clear that the sort of person the prisoner became was the result of an inner decision, and not the result of camp influences alone. Fundamentally, therefore, any man can, even under such circumstances, decide what shall become of him—mentally and spiritually. He may retain his human dignity even in a concentration camp. Dostoevsky said once, "There is only one thing that I dread: not to be worthy of my sufferings."*

Amidst the inhumanity and degradation of the camps, Frankl came face to face with a fundamental and unavoidable fact of life: Whether in the horrors of Auschwitz or in the day-to-day routine of our pedestrian lives, "to live is to suffer, (and) to survive is to find meaning in the suffering."[8] For Frankl the meaning of life *includes* suffering, privation, and death.

All of us suffer in life, said Frankl. Some of us suffer physical pain, oppression, torture, and poverty. Others of us suffer boredom, emptiness, ennui. For Frankl, it is really a question of degree, not kind. For him, the Nazi camps were just the most radical and absurd example of the pain and suffering humans can experience in life. The simple, unavoidable fact is that life is a struggle for everyone. Injustice and unfairness are a part of the human condition. Frankl suggests that life may not be a penalty, but it is a contest that we can choose to affect and influence.

To ask Job's question—"Why did this happen to me?"—is futile, for no answer exists. One must accept that injustice, chance, arbitrariness, and evil do exist. If "there is a meaning in life at all, then there must be a meaning in the suffering."[9] Frankl argues that even in the most restrictive circumstances we can use our freedom, even if only minimally, to influence our actions… or at the least our attitude toward what is happening to us. He wrote:

A human being is not one thing among others; things determine each other, but [people are] ultimately self-determining. What [we become]—within the limits of endowment and environment—[we have] made out of [ourselves]. In the concentration camps, for example, in this living laboratory and on this testing ground, we watched and witnessed some of our comrades behave like swine, while others behaved like saints. [People have] both potentialities within [themselves]; which one is actualized depends on decisions but not on conditions. [10]

As a catholic philosopher, I am drawn to Victor Frankl's text because his message is so human, so fundamental, so universal. As a species, long before we concern ourselves with formal academic questions regarding metaphysics, epistemology, or even ethics, we are drawn to a much more immediate and personal philosophical question: What is the meaning of life? Or, more precisely: What is the meaning of *my* life? Drawing on his experiences in the cruel "laboratory" of the camps, Frankl is convinced that even in the face of senseless and arbitrary death we humans are constant seekers of a purpose, a cause, a belief larger than ourselves.

The camps taught Frankl that the only way to endure the atrocities of his surroundings was to have a dream to believe in, a goal to achieve, a task to complete. Frankl endured because he nurtured the hope, the dream, the desperate desire that he might survive long enough to see his wife again. Each day he tried to recall her smile, the sound of her voice, the little gestures he once took for granted that were now treasured memories of domestic delight. Once, when he thought he was about to be "selected" for extermination, he asked a fellow prisoner to take a message to his wife. He told the man:

Listen, Otto, if I don't get back home to my wife, and if you should see her again, then tell her that I talked of her daily, hourly. You remem-

ber. Secondly, I have loved her more than anyone. Thirdly, the short time I have been married to her outweighs everything, even all we have gone through here.[11]

I still contend that there is no one single philosophy book that can itemize and address all or even most of the salient issues and questions regarding the human condition. Nevertheless, if I have to pick just one, it is Frankl's, because it is so basic, so vital, so "catholic." He conceived it while undergoing an experience far, far worse (because it was real) than Dante's fictional depiction of the "third circle of hell" or Job's rise and fall and rise from grace. For Frankl, Auschwitz was a cruel teacher, but one that taught him (and us) these crucial life lessons:

1. Without meaning, our lives are diminished, deficient, and dysfunctional.

2. "He who has a why to live for, can endure any how!" (Nietzsche)

3. Even when people have nothing left in this world, they may still know bliss, if only for a moment, in the contemplations of their beloved.

4. "That which does not kill me, makes me stronger." (Nietzsche)

Man's Search for Meaning should not be the only philosophy book a person ever reads; but it is, I think, a perfect one with which to begin…and to end.

IV

Too Many Changes, Too Many Choices

We need to teach the next generation of children from Day One that they are responsible for their lives. Mankind's greatest gift, also its greatest curse, is that we have free choice. We can make our choices built from love or from fear.

Elisabeth Kübler-Ross

If Viktor Frankl discovered that humans *always* have a choice, philosophers also point out that we can have too many changes and choices in our lives, and that it's not always easy figuring out what's the right thing to do.

Twenty-five hundred years ago, when the iron hoe was an important new invention in the world, the pre-Socratic philosophers of Greece conjectured on the metaphysical substructure of reality. For Pythagoras, math was the logic, language, and glue of the cosmos. For Thales, the stuff of life was water. For Anaximenes, it was air. For Anaximander, it was the forces of hot and cold. And for Heraclitus, the fundamental element of life was change. Heraclitus noted that nothing is permanent; flux or change is everywhere. Reality is flux, permanency is not possible, and the only constant is change.

Even if change does not constitute the metaphysical and philosophical building blocks of reality, psychologically Heraclitus's general thesis is compelling and seemingly self-evident to both reason and the senses. If things are always changing, if nothing is ever final or fixed, then all of life, all of truth, is not necessarily relative but is in process, evolution, and development. If change is the essential activity of experience, then all that we witness and know is continuously being redefined, reshaped, and even altered. Change does not mean that there is *no thing*. It does mean that all things are in motion, that nothing steadfastly *is*. It means all things are forever being modified, and that reality is constantly changing and augmenting itself. Heraclitus saw change as the lubricant and catalyst of life. Change is the *medium* if not the *message* of life.

At both the biological and social level, change is to the human condition what water is to a fish. It is the milieu we live in. Like time, change means continuous movement, newness, novelty. As part of the human condition, change is not optional, artificial, or personal. Some forms of change are threatening. Some forms are unfair, others are beneficial. Some forms are positive and offer a new chance or opportunity. But good, bad, or indifferent, change is inevitable.

Alvin Toffler has correctly pointed out that the central issue of the postmodern era is not just change, but rather the increased pace and rate of change in our lives. Toffler believes, and most of us will attest, that we are presently experiencing more change than ever before, and that we are experiencing the change at an accelerated rate.

If there is one absolute in regard to change, it is that change can and does bring about new situations and problems that can't always be solved and answered with the same old solutions. Neither Aristotle, Albert the Great, Immanuel Kant, nor John Stuart Mill directly spoke to the complexities and nuances of heart transplant surgery, genetic research, global warming, industrial pollution, leveraged buyouts, hostile takeover bids, and women in the workplace. Each generation in turn finds itself confronted with issues and ideas that preceding generations never imagined. Each generation must address the issues of its age, often using vocabularies of thought and methodologies specially created to confront the issue at hand. As Albert Einstein so eloquently phrased it, "The significant problems we face cannot be solved at the same level of thinking we were at when we created them."

～

Directly connected to the problem of the increasing pace and rate of change in our lives is the increasing number and variety of choices we are forced to make in our lives. Albert Camus once asked the questions, "Should I kill myself, or have a cup of coffee?" I believe that this quote is nothing more than a dramatic, tongue-in-cheek, existential reminder that everything we do in life is a choice, and that all of human existence and our very essence (our definition as a person) is literally defined by the choices we make.

Clearly, one need not be a card-carrying existentialist to agree with Camus on this point. Life *is* full of choices. Some of the choices we face are critical, and many more of them are utterly unimportant. But choose we must. We are, in fact, a species of choosers, and we are known and defined by the quality of the choices we make.

As social theorist Barry Schwartz writes in *The Paradox of Choice: Why More Is Less*, choices and choosing are psychologically a crucial part of the human condition. Making choices and the freedom to make choices is how human beings express their autonomy, develop self-respect and self-worth, and achieve self-definition. Freedom of choice is a core value politically as well, says Schwartz. The United States was founded on a commitment to individual freedom and autonomy. Politically and economically, freedom allows people to choose, to risk, to take a chance, to extend themselves to improve the quality of their lives. According to Schwartz, people want and need to direct their own lives. Choices keep us growing and offer us the possibilities of creature comforts, greater levels of awareness, and creativity. When there are no choices, life can become uniform, utterly uninteresting, and unbearable.

But, says Schwartz, when the number of choices keeps *growing*, there is a downside. He argues that just because some choice is good, it doesn't mean that *more* choice is always better. Too many choices can lead to overload, anxiety, stress, dissatisfaction, bad decision making, and even clinical depression. For Schwartz, at some point, too many choices no longer liberates but, rather, debilitates. In fact, too many choices can tyrannize our lives.

Schwartz says that he started his research on the burden of choice when he innocently went into a Gap store to buy a pair of jeans. He said, "I want a pair of jeans—32-27." The saleswoman said: "Slim fit? Easy fit? Relaxed fit? Baggy or extra baggy? Do you want stonewashed? Or how about unwashed or acid wash? Do you want them faded or regular? How about a button-fly or a zipper-fly?" He said, "Huh? I just want regular jeans. You know, the kind that used to be the only kind." She said, "Regular jeans? Let me go ask somebody."[1]

Ultimately, Schwartz did get his jeans. But in the process he had an epiphany that turned into a hypothesis, which six years later turned into a book. "The jeans I chose turned out just fine, but it occurred to me that day that buying a pair of pants should not be a day-long project. By creating all these options, the store undoubtedly had done a favor to customers with varied tastes and body types. However, by vastly expanding the range of choices, they had also created a new problem that needed to be solved. Before these options were available...purchasing jeans was a five-minute affair. Now it was a complex decision in which I was forced to invest time, energy, and no small amount of self-doubt, anxiety, and dread."[2]

Schwartz argues that our culture has sanctified the freedom of choice so profoundly that we believe the benefits of infinite options are self-evident.[3] (The Internet has made our options almost literally infinite.) My parents lived in an economic system that struggled through the optionless Depression era and survived the social sacrifices and economic parsimony necessary to win two major world wars. Until recently, however, my generation and those who followed have seemed to live by the motto, "If some is good, more is better!" The collapse of the economy in 2008-2010 may have brought some sanity regarding the limitations of resources back into our society, or it may prove to be just a temporary blip on our road to limitless choice.

At a certain point, says Schwartz, increased complexity in regard to choices does not lead to increased satisfaction. In fact, the reverse often occurs. We experience a diminishment of self and satisfaction when we are confronted with too many choices to make concerning too many options. From groceries to cars, clothing, insurance policies, retirement plans, cable carriers, cell-phone packages and rates—the options never seem to end and we wind up exhausted and confused by the number of choices we need to make on a daily basis.

The problem, Schwartz writes, isn't just *this* particular choice over *that* particular choice. We now face more choices and decisions today than ever before, and the cumulative effect of all these added choices demands too much of our time, attention, and energy. It is also the case, says Schwartz, that more choices simply present new things to worry about, to master, or perhaps to get wrong.

From a philosophical point of view, true freedom cannot be equated simply with a surfeit of options and choices. True freedom, or the primary purpose of freedom, is to have the opportunity and ability to make good choices about things that really matter. Yes, it's important to choose a good breakfast cereal, a dependable car, an effective household soap, an efficient showerhead, and a trustworthy health insurance policy. But when we must choose from two-hundred-and-fifty cereals, ten models of basically the same car, forty soaps, thirty-five showerheads, and five-hundred insurance policies we often find ourselves not only exhausted but also disengaged and distracted from more important decisions and choices in our lives. As Schwartz sagely suggests, time spent dealing with consumer choices and ephemeral choices of all kinds is time taken away from choosing to be a good friend, a good spouse, a good parent, or a good person.[4]

What Schwartz's book suggests to me is that too many of the choices we make within our capitalistic culture lock us into a purely parochial and self-serving perspective on reality. These choices reinforce our narcissistic tendencies and insulate us from others. Over time, the volume of choices that we face can anesthetize us to any issue that stands outside of the shadow of self. In the pursuit of too many choices, we are diminished and incomplete. In our preoccupation with self-aggrandizement, we lose ourselves in choices that contribute little or nothing to the matters that truly nourish us, enhance our self-respect, or enable us to participate in community life.

Martin Heidegger, in his philosophical critique of the human condition, *Being and Time*, suggests that—in lieu of being able to address the serious choices, questions, and issues in life—we often busy ourselves in idle play, cocktail party conversations, and/or escapist behavior. In American society, of course, the escapist behavior of choice is shopping. In this society we "communicate with commodities."[5] People find comfort in and recognize themselves in their possessions. The seductive siren call of the ad cult industry continually bombards us with a message that is both mystic and metaphysical: "Can't figure out the ultimate questions in life? Don't sweat it! We've got them figured out for you. You *can* buy happiness. You *can* be loved. You *can* be accepted. You *can* be transformed into the person you want to be. Just buy our product and keep buying it until we come up with another product we will make you feel you want and need."

Vaclav Havel, the former Czechoslovakian president and playwright, warns us of the spiritual and moral disease engendering by a "choice-filled" consumer culture. Shopping he says, is "a desperate substitute for living." When life "becomes reduced to a hunt for consumer goods," freedom becomes trivialized to mean "a chance to freely choose which washing machine or refrigerator we want to buy." Consumer bliss, Havel points out, diverts people's attention from the community itself. A consumer culture makes it easy to accept the slow erosion of social, political, and moral standards because their passing is hardly noticed—we're all too busy shopping.[6]

Though the diagnosis is dire, a cure is yet possible. As Barry Schwartz succinctly puts it, we must learn "to make good choices about things that matter, while at the same time unburdening ourselves from too much concern about things that don't."[7] This is, of course, a task easier said than done.

Change is a basic fact of life. Good, bad, or ugly change is a natural and continuous process. Change is neither an aberration nor a personal assault.

The popular philosophical formula for this is "shit happens." (For you Latin scholars, that would of course be "*stercus accidit*.") The reality is that change does alter, augment, and restructure the world around us. Change affects the currency and credibility of our ideas and values. Change also forces us to reevaluate or at least revisit some of our long-held beliefs and conventions.

Choice, on the other hand, is an intentional act. Choice is something we decide to do. Choice is something we, presumably, want to do. What choice is really about, from a philosophical point of view, is human freedom and moral courage (the subject of the next chapter); and all catholic philosophers (both upper and lowercase) have always been on that particular train.

It would, of course, be easy or, at least, a lot easier to make choices— ethical or otherwise—if they occurred in a vacuum free of variables, without change or outside influence. But clearly, such is not the case. And so the challenge all of us face is to try to cope with change while managing our ethical priorities and moral sense of self.

Chapter V
The Seven Deadly Sins

You are dust,
and to dust you shall return.

Genesis 2:19

The downside of freedom and choice, of course, is that we humans often choose badly. In Catholicism, we call this "sin." We even differentiate sin in several ways. Some sins are "venial," meaning "not that bad," and some are "mortal," meaning "get your butt to confession." We also have sins of "commission," which are bad things we do (or things we do badly), and sins of "omission," which are things we fail to do (like bringing about the Kingdom of God on earth as it is in heaven). Ironically, we are both attracted to and repulsed by the concept of sin. Allow me to explain.

We humans are a glorious species, and we know it. Individually and collectively we have achieved wondrous things, scaled great heights, performed heroic deeds. We have harnessed the powers of the sun, discovered cures for age-old maladies, and produced machines that can literally and virtually take us to the moon and beyond. We are indeed an interesting and amazing collection of protoplasm. And yet for all of our success, we know we are also a race of scoundrels, scallywags, and rapscallions. The Catholic Church says we are all sinners and doomed because of the misbehavior of the first human couple in the Garden of Eden. Their sin became our heritage. We are, says Luther, born "full of evil lusts and inclinations from our mothers' wombs."[1] And so, says St. Augustine, our propagation is therefore "vitiated by sin" and we are "bound by the chain of death, and justly condemned."[2] Sages and scholars have also pointed out that we are a vainglorious, weak breed. We succumb too easily to our passions, our wants, our debauched desires. Between the failings of the flesh and the selfishness of the psyche, more often than not, we are driven by our appetites rather than our reason.

Because of all this, philosophers of almost every persuasion have agreed that we are in need of rules, regulations, commandments, and moral codes to steady our course and find a middle ground between Dionysian excess and Spartan frugality.

Pope Gregory I (540-604 AD) earned the moniker of "the Great" in part due to his prodigious personal work ethic and the collective efforts of his curia and staff during his fourteen-year reign as Supreme Pontiff, during what historians call the "Dark Ages." Just for starters, his papacy is credited with the reorganization of the bureaucratic structure of the Church and the establishment of the Gregorian chant (named after himself, of course) as its official liturgical music. (Gregory the Great was not, however, the author of the Gregorian calendar. That accomplishment can be credited to Pope Gregory XIII in 1582—almost 1,000 years later—who unfortunately missed the actual date of Jesus' birth by several years.)

Gregory I was not the first clerical thinker to articulate a catalogue of "cardinal" or "capital" sins. The earliest attempts at creating a list of the most serious sins had it origin in the monastic movement of the Eastern Church. The fourth-century Egyptian monk Evasrius of Pontas originally defined eight deadly sins, and it was the ascetic John Cassian of Marseilles who introduced this list to Western monasticism at the time of Gregory the Great.

Before becoming pope, Gregory had lived the life of a monk and at one time was abbot of the monastery of St. Andrew's in Italy. Cerebral, austere, and ascetic by nature, Gregory was drawn to this list, because, in part, he saw in it an opportunity to address the fundamental "vices besetting the monastic life," as he put it.[3] In creating and promulgating his final list of the seven biggest sins, Gregory hoped to offer a tool for contemplation that would help maintain the ascetic regimen of a monk's life as well as reinforce the essential monastic vows of chastity, poverty, and obedience. Gregory was aware, however, that the temptations and vices of the monastery were not limited to those living a cloistered lifestyle. All people, he declared, needed to be reminded of the temptations of the world and the need for constant vigilance, simplicity, and sanctity. Gregory offered his list of the "seven deadly sins" to "serve as a classification of the normal perils of the soul in the ordinary conditions of life."[4]

Each of the seven sins, suggested Gregory, offered us an opportunity to concentrate on the evil and vice of sin, while at the same time meditating on the virtue and beneficence of its opposite. His list of the seven sins and their corresponding virtues looked something like this:

Sin/Vice	Latin Name	Better Known Today	Corresponding Virtue
Pride	*Superbia*	Vanity, Ego-Tripping	Humility
Envy	*Invidia*	Jealousy, Entitlement	Love
Anger	*Ira*	Rage, Fury, Wrath, Hatred	Kindness
Sloth	*Acedia*	Whining, Laziness, Idleness	Zeal
Avarice	*Avaritia*	Greed, Materialism, Covetousness	Generosity
Gluttony	*Gula*	Addiction, Overindulgence	Temperance
Lust	*Luxuria*	Excessive Physical Desire, Obsession	Self-Control

ᔕ

Why seven? Was Gregory guilty of *hebdomania* (an obsession with the number seven or sets of seven)? Why not *ten* sins to complement the Ten Commandments? And why these seven? Why not a longer list of damnable, dangerous, and destructive sins? Maybe the "Top 100 Sins of All-Time"? After all, says ethicist Bob Solomon, "among the many man-made evils in the world, the deadly seven barely jiggle the scales of justice, and it is hard to imagine why God would bother to raise a celestial eyebrow about them."[5] Clearly, Gregory could have come up with a list of vices eminently more vile and vicious than this pedestrian seven. For example, Solomon asks, why didn't "human viciousness and brutality, cruelty, savagery, indifference to human suffering, tyranny, ethical hatred, religious persecution and/or racial bigotry" make the list?[6]

The genius and brilliance of Gregory's list (and what made him great, at least on this matter) is precisely that his choices are so pedestrian, so commonplace, so—in the words of Friedrich Nietzsche—"human-all-too-human." The seven deadly sins bespeak the most common of human errors and frailties. These seven "are not rare violations or the total break down of civility, they are routine and mundane features of human behavior."[7] There is nothing new or novel in this list. Who among us has not wrestled with moments of exaggerated self-importance (pride), bowel-churning resentment in regard to the good fortune of others (envy), and irrational feelings of hatred or revenge (anger)? Which of us has not rebuked ourselves for being excessively lazy (sloth) or for wanting too much (greed)? Who of us has not chided ourselves for overeating (gluttony), or for having impure thoughts in regard to an inappropriate other (lust)? These sins and failings are not just philosophical abstractions debated and discussed in a classroom. These are issues of the human heart and the human condition. Times, symptoms, and fashions may change, but each generation must deal with these perennial matters.

There is, I think, another fundamental reason why Gregory stressed this deadly septet. If we cannot control or correct our most "common" sins and failings, how will we be able to handle and master larger and more destructive temptations and vices? How are we to avoid sin, if the repetition of sin engenders sin? In the thirteenth century, the "Angelic Doctor," Thomas Aquinas, embraced and endorsed Gregory's list specifically on this point. Thomas argues that Gregory's list of vices "are those that give rise to others." Sin, suggested Thomas, creates the inclination and desire to sin again. And this perverse inclination clouds our consciousness and corrupts our concrete judgment in regard to good and evil. Sins are the "workers of woe."[8] They begit and begat each other and truly take over one's soul. In the words and warning of Augustine of Hippo: *"Peccatum poena peccati"*—"Sin is the punishment of sin." For Gregory, Aquinas, and Augustine these seemingly parochial sins were common enough yet grievous and deadly enough to test "God's infinite capacity for forgiveness," specifically because they encouraged and reinforced two of our greatest weaknesses as a species: narcissistic self-adsorption and the pleasures of the flesh.

Spiritually, at its core, sin is about disobedience and denial. It is about turning away from God (and all others) in the pursuit of one's own sense of needs, wants, and desires. The essential hubris of sin is that we become our own self-serving God in the pursuit of our own hedonistic predilections. When we sin, we deem ourselves *sui generis*. We deem our actions and desires as self-evident and self-justified. We see the world as both an obstacle and an opportunity. We determine all of our decisions and actions exclusively based on our own parochial narcissistic perspective. According to literary scholar Newton Arvin, the essential sin of narcissism is that it shuts up the spirit—the soul—in a dungeon where it is alone and beyond the reach of God and others. Narcissism creates a solipsistic universe that both isolates and damns us.

In spite of the efforts of Karl Menninger in 1973 with his book *Whatever Became of Sin?* to revive the concept of sin as a positive heuristic and psychological mechanism for the development of personal and social ethical standards, the passage of time has witnessed the erosion of the concept and discussion of sin. According to theologian George Otis, sin has even lost its prominence and popularity as a sermon theme.[9] We still hear sermons on moral defects, misdeeds, and topics revolving around the concepts of social justice and personal integrity, but the concept of sin now carries with it a certain archaic medieval quality. Even in the official *Catechism of the Catholic Church*, consisting of 2,865 numbered sections and first published in 1992 by order of Pope John Paul II, the seven deadly sins are dealt with in a single paragraph.[10]

Numerous critics have also suggested that in a media-driven, economically interconnected, postmodern society, Gregory's code is ironically and shockingly non-catholic (as in the Latin *catholicus*—"universal, whole, comprehensive"), highly subjective, and outdated in nature. According to a 2005 poll commissioned by the British Broadcasting Company (BBC), the British public no longer believes that Gregory's list of sins has any relevance to their lives. They have offered a new up-to-date list of cardinal sins that more closely reflects our global state of electronic, economic, and ecological interdependence and inter-connectedness. The new list only incorporates one of the original seven deadlies—(greed), and it offers cruelty as the worst modern-day sin, followed by adultery, bigotry, dishonesty, hypocrisy, greed, and selfishness.[11] What the survey is suggesting is that these new sins are not solitary activities whose impact is always limited and unilateral. These are sins that always involve others and can have deleterious efforts on many. These are sins that reflect the radically intertwined nature of modern life.

It is also interesting to note that Mohandas Karamchand Gandhi, in his struggles for the rights and dignity of the Indian people and their then newly organized state, also argued that all virtues and vices must be measured and weighed in relation to their impact on others and not solely on the self. For Gandhi, there is no such thing as "a person" living "a life" totally distinct and detached from others. For Gandhi, sin is always measured in regard to others. Consequently, his list might be more accurately entitled the Seven Most Deadly Social Sins.

TWO NEW LISTS OF SEVEN DEADLIES

BBC Poll	Mahatma Gandhi
Cruelty	Wealth without work
Adultery	Pleasure without conscience
Bigotry	Science without humanity
Dishonesty	Knowledge without character
Hypocrisy	Politics without principles
Greed	Commerce without morality
Selfishness	Worship without sacrifice

In 2008, the Vatican formally added to Gregory the Great's original list when it published Benedict XVI's "New Seven Deadly Sins."

THE NEW SUGGESTED SEVEN

Pope Benedict XVI
Genetic modification
Human experiments, such as cloning
Polluting the environment
Causing social injustice
Causing poverty
Becoming obscenely wealthy
Taking drugs

In a press conference, Vatican spokesman Cardinal Gianfranco Girotti said that the Church found it necessary to offer a broader range of sins that better reflects the challenges and temptations of the modern age. "Attention

to sin is a more urgent task today," said Girotti, "precisely because its consequences are more abundant and destructive." The new reality is "you offend
God not only by stealing, blasphemy, or coveting your neighbor's wife, but
also by polluting, cloning, taking drugs, promoting social injustice, or becoming obscenely rich. Where the standard sins are individual failings, in a
global culture, sin is social."[12]

To be fair, to say that Gregory's nasty seven are solitary, totally self-
contained, and without any larger social consequences is to be naive about
how individual human wants, needs, and desires are publicly pursued, played
out, and fulfilled. As psychotherapist Solomon Schimmel has suggested, the
pursuit of any one of the seven necessarily fuels and spawns larger harmful
social phenomena: lust—pornography; gluttony—substance abuse; envy—
terrorism; anger—violence; sloth—indifference to the pain and suffering of
others; greed—abuse of public trust; and pride—discrimination.[13]

Whether you completely agree with Gregory's list or not, at the level of
popular culture, the seven deadly sins have endured the test of time and have
been traditionally used as a personal and societal barometer of moral health
and fitness. Like Karl Menniger, Gregory wanted to support and encourage
the study of sin in order "to identify it, to define it, to warn us about it, and to
spur measures for combating and rectifying it."[14] For Gregory, understanding sin, understanding that we are sinners, is a summons to life, growth, and
betterment. In being able to recognize the nature, reality, and severity of our
sins, we give ourselves the opportunity to re-adjust our moral compass.

Even those who are not religious intuitively understand the concept of
sin. Sin is about "doing wrong," "the willful violation of rules and standards,"
"offenses against propriety." Sin is about harm to one's self as well as harm
to one's relationship with others. Sinning is the violation of tribal or community laws and customs. Sinning is about the loss of control. Sinning is
about excesses and deficiencies in interactions with others. Sinning is about
"estrangement"—from self, others, one's community, and one's God (how-

ever that reality is understood or described or denied). Sinning leads to the diminishment of self physically, psychologically, and spiritually. Perhaps the greatest penalty of sin, next to turning us away from the face of God, is that it renders us less than fully human, less than fully functioning, and not attuned to the real needs of self and the rights of others.

At the most practical level, Robert C. Solomon argues that the deadly sins have as much to do with poor health as they do with damnation and moral degeneracy. The bottom line, says Solomon, is that what is deadly about the deadly sins is that they lead to a reduced lifespan, bad health, an unpleasant appearance, and the inability to attract and sustain either friends or mates. Just think about it for a minute, gluttony is really a code name for calories, high cholesterol, and obesity. Lust can involve unsafe sex and the risk of AIDS. Sloth means not getting enough exercise. Greed is about overdoing it, taking on more than you can handle, addictive behavior. Pride leads us to believing that bad things only happen to other people, so we don't have to worry about the consequences of our bad behavior. So, why cut back? Indulge yourself. Enjoy! Envy can become an excuse for indifference, apathy, not trying. And anger can lead to combative behavior, black eyes, and high blood pressure.[15]

Philosophically speaking, the seven sins are in fact *deadly* precisely because their "apparent innocuousness," their "insidious subversiveness," their "undeniable ordinariness"[16] erodes our critical skills and anesthetizes our ethical sensitivities. Thus we need to take the seven deadly sins seriously, not just because they involve occasional acts of wrongdoing, but because the habit of doing wrong—the habit of repeated transgressions—has a major influence on the formulation of self-identity and moral character. And as Heraclites so eloquently pointed out, "One's character shapes one's fate."

The editor of the Oxford University Press series on the seven deadly sins, Elda Rotor, has pointed out that Gregory's fifteen-hundred-year-old list has been the catalyst for innumerable debates, doctoral defenses, documentaries, plays, novels, jokes, and cartoons. The deadly seven have been championed, challenged, discussed, and dissected by a long list of luminaries: Aquinas, Dante, Chaucer, Rousseau, Montaigne, Hobbes, Hume, Mandeville, Poe, Kafka, Mencken, Faulkner, Maugham, and Leone. The nugget of truth at the bottom of all of this, for Rotor, is clear: Our contemporary fascination with, our struggle against, and our celebration of these age-old sins tells us much about our continued desire to better define and understand our earthly human condition as well as our aspirations to achieve the divine.[17]

The teachings of Gregory the Great remind us just how degrading, destructive, and delicious sin can be. Because we are frail owing to the human condition, we are easily drawn to the temptations and the shallow, transitory comforts of sin. For Gregory, the seven deadly sins represented the most pedestrian and perhaps the most "venial" of transgressions. But, as he suggested, they are "the trunk of the tree from which (all) other (sins) branch."[18] Their simplicity makes them seductive, and with each seduction the sinner is led further down the slippery slope toward apostasy and damnation.

For Gregory, the avoidance of sin can only come from knowledge, contemplation, and virtue—the ability and habit of making good choices. In formulating his seven deadliest list, he was admonishing and warning his flock that we cannot "compartmentalize our lives" and think that we can get away with an occasional lapse or fall from grace and yet maintain our character. Sinning is like lying. Each successful lie makes the next one easier. And the habit of lying leads to the eradication of truth and integrity. I do not think that Gregory's purpose was to scare us. His purpose, I think, was primarily to present another way of resolving the Socratic quest: "An unexamined life is not worth living."

Chapter VI

A Short Primer on Moral Courage

I wanted you to see what real courage is, instead of getting the idea that courage is a man with a gun in his hand. It's when you know you're licked before you begin but your begin anyway and you see it through no matter what.

Harper Lee

The opposite of sin, of course, is virtue, and from a catholic philosopher's point of view, the most interesting virtue is moral courage.

In a colloquial sense, the concept of courage is usually associated with physical acts of daring-do that involve danger, risk, and behavior that overcomes seemingly insurmountable obstacles and odds. The word *courage* conjures up images of individuals performing difficult actions while risking physical injury or death. A courageous act is one in which the actor disregards concern for personal safety or well-being and exerts himself or herself in the service of others. The courageous act is thus seen as the heroic act. In popular culture, we use the word *hero* to honor soldiers, firefighters, rescue workers, and others who do what they do with little regard for their own safety. From this perspective, courage is a super-virtue, an extraordinary achievement, and not part of the common repertoire of traits and behaviors associated with the more mundane and pedestrian aspects of our lives.

From a psychoanalytic perspective, however, Ernest Becker, in his classic text, *The Denial of Death*, deconstructs our commonsensical definition of courage to mean not an altruistic concern for others but rather a myopic preoccupation with self. Becker argues that the "primary mainspring" of human action is not the pursuit of sex, as Freud proposed, but rather the pursuit of "distractions" that will counterbalance our overwhelming fear of the immensity of eternity and the awareness of our finitude. As a species, says Becker, human beings have a basic existential dilemma: We are both burdened and blessed with a paradoxical nature, half animal and half symbolic. That means that we are simultaneously aware of the *possibility* of infinity and the absolute *certainty* that we are finite. We live our whole lifetimes, said Becker, with the "fate of death haunting our dreams" even on the "most sun-filled days."[1]

The idea of death, says Becker, the fear of it, haunts us like nothing else. It is the "motivating principle" of human activity. And all human activity is consciously and unconsciously designed to deny and combat our fear and terror of death.[2] The "painful riddle of death" haunts us, he says, causing us mental and physical grief and despair. Our fear wears us out, and so out of necessity we seek to repress it, sublimate it, take it off the table of our immediate sense of consciousness. We create mental defenses, illusions, myths, stories, tasks, crusades, causes, work, rituals, and bizarre behaviors to distract us from our discomfort and despair. Becker writes that the most dramatic way to deny the terror of death is to act as if fear means nothing to us and that we are not helpless and abandoned in the world and fated for oblivion. If we cannot beat death, we can at least temporarily ignore and deny it through culturally-sanctioned heroic acts as well as by outrageous acts of violence and evil. For Becker, it is only in choosing to act that we assert our "being" and, at least temporarily, overcome "nothingness." Heroism, he writes, "is first and foremost a reflex of terror and death. We admire most the courage to face death; we give such valor our highest and most constant adoration; it moves us deeply in our hearts because we have doubts about how brave we ourselves would be…. [Humans have] elevated animal courage to a cult."[3]

Becker argues that the "hero project" is a pose, a learned character trait, a grand illusion, and a "neurotic defense against despair."[4] In the "hero project," we put on the "character armor" (William Reich's term) of the action hero, "lay away" our fears, and pretend to make the world more manageable.

Like William James' notion of "acting oneself into being," the hero, through his or her actions, seeks reinforcement of self, recognition, unabashed self-esteem, ersatz immortality, and, if possible, cosmic significance. For Becker, heroic acts are neither selfless nor sincere. They are, rather, sublimated forms of escapist behavior. (Perhaps this is why athletes are often held up, or hold themselves up, to be heroes in modern society. Their "courage" is mistaken for the real thing.)

For the philosopher, physical courage in and of itself is not that interesting. Very few professional athletes, for example, are philosophers (with the possible exception of Yogi Berra), and likewise we philosophers are not usually noted for our acts of physical courage. (Hence the image of the "ivory tower" professor who doesn't even know what is happening on the street below.)

But we are fascinated by a particular form of courage: *moral* courage, at least from a philosophical and ethical point of view. We tend to agree with Winston Churchill: "Courage is the first of human qualities because it is the quality which guarantees all others."

Moral courage is not an "extra" or a "supernumerary" virtue but rather a critical human quality that serves as a necessary precondition for all other forms of moral conduct. Moral courage is the readiness to endure danger for the sake of principle.[5] Moral courage rejects voyeurism and seeks engagement. Moral courage is a stimulus, a catalyst for action. As Nelson Mandela has suggested, moral courage is not the absence of fear but the strength to triumph over one's fear and to act.[6] Moral courage is the ability to transcend fear and endure risk for principle. It is the ability to put ethics into actual practice. And that is why it fascinates philosophers.

The central problem for humanity today is not a lack of moral reasoning or moral imagination—we've got those in spades in our colleges and universities—but rather a lack of moral engagement or moral courage.[7] By that I mean a lack of willingness to take on ethical issues and questions, to extend ourselves, to put ourselves in harm's way because we are concerned about the well-being of others.

Publicly, we may live lives that are economically and electronically interconnected and interdependent, but privately we are emotionally and ethically withdrawn, unappreciative, and unempathetic to the wants, needs, and desires of others. If we care about anyone else at all, it is only after we have first taken care of our own self-centered wants and needs.

I believe that ethics is possible only when we are able to step away from ourselves or, to borrow a phrase, "to forget about ourselves on purpose."[8] We must be able to see beyond our self-contained universe of personal concerns. We must be able to become, if only momentarily, more selfless than selfish.

Sören Kierkegaard said that "subjectivity is the starting point of ethics." But subjectivity is neither the end point nor the only point of ethics. Ethics begins with the recognition that we are not alone or the center of the universe. It is always about self in the context of others. It must be open to the voice of others. Being ethical begins with having the courage to stand outside of the needs of self and listen to others and act on their behalf.

Without moral courage to propel us forward, we become captives of our own needs and desires. Getting free of self, overcoming our natural tendency to be self-absorbed in our interactions with others, is the central problem and paradox of communal existence and therefore a central question in philosophy and ethics. Although the term "narcissism" or "narcissistic type" is not often used in philosophical circles, I think it should be. The concept of narcissism neatly encapsulates the dark side of why it is so hard to get free of what I call the "shadow of self."

The narcissist does not see past the needs and wants of self. According to the *Synopsis of Psychiatry*, persons with narcissistic personality disorder are characterized by a heightened sense of self-importance and grandiose feelings that they are unique in some way. They consider themselves special people and expect special treatment. They always want their own way and are frequently ambitious, desiring fame and fortune. Their relationships with others are fragile and limited. They are unable to show empathy and feign sympathy with others only to achieve their own ends. Interpersonal exploitation is commonplace. The narcissist is totally absorbed in the shadow of self and either cannot or will not focus on or imagine the needs of others.[9]

Ethical decision making requires us to look beyond the immediate moment and beyond personal needs, desires, and wants in order to *imagine* the possible consequences of our decisions and behavior on ourselves and others. In its most elemental sense, moral imagination is about picturing various outcomes in our interactions with others. In some sense, moral imagination is a dramatic virtual rehearsal that allows us to examine and appraise different courses of action in order to determine the morally best thing to do. The capacity for empathy is crucial to moral imagination. As Adam Smith wrote, "As we have no immediate experience of what [others] feel, we can form no idea of the manner in which they are affected, but by conceiving what we ourselves should feel in the situation."[10]

According to philosopher Patricia H. Werhane of DePaul University, the failure of this capacity—the inability to imagine and to be sympathetic to the needs, passions, and interests of others—is the main cause of moral ineptitudes. Werhane writes that to sympathize is to place myself in another's situation, "not because of how that situation might affect me, but rather if I were that person, in that situation."[11] Being imaginative, using "moral imagination," allows us to be self-reflective and step back from our situation so as to see it from another point of view. In taking such a perspective, says Werhane, a person tries to look at the world or himself or herself from the point of view of a dispassionate, reasonable person who is not wholly absorbed with self. Werhane calls this transpositional perspective "a disengaged view from somewhere," and within it a number of questions become obligatory:

1. What would a reasonable person judge is the right thing to do?
2. Could one defend this decision publicly?
3. What kind of precedent does this decision set?
4. Is this decision or action necessary?
5. Is this the least-worst option?[12]

What Werhane is suggesting is that one must, in making an ethical decision, determine the answers to some crucial questions: What's at stake? What are the issues? Who else is involved? And what are the alternatives? Moral imagination allows us the possibility of addressing these questions from a perspective that is both inside and outside the box, a perspective that focuses on self and others.

Without the ability to see beyond the needs of self, we treat the rest of the world as other, as irrelevant, as inconsequential. This leitmotif completely ignores a whole series of questions. What are our obligations to the great sea of others, our neighbors? Are we obligated to help neighbors when doing so is reasonable and does not entail a serious inconvenience or risk of harm? Are we obligated to help neighbors where the price we pay may include the risk of great danger and/or inconvenience? Are we required to endanger ourselves for our neighbors? Finally, do we at least have a minimal responsibility to help our neighbors? What about strangers? And people who live in other parts of the world? And generations to come? And aliens if we ever encounter them?

On March 13, 1964, at 3:15 a.m. on a brisk winter morning along a quiet, picturesque, respectable, tree-lined street in Kew Gardens of Queens, New York City, Catherine "Kitty" Genovese, the twenty-eight-year-old daughter of middle-class Italian-American parents, was brutally stabbed to death. There are at least three factors that make Kitty Genovese's murder especially heinous and unforgettable. To begin with, it was a random act that occurred without rhyme or reason (the killer was simply out roaming the streets looking for a "little action.") The second startling aspect of this crime was its sheer brutality. In the course of three separate stabbing events, which lasted over thirty-five minutes, Kitty endured at least seventeen wounds. Finally, and the most horribly, Kitty Genovese's cries and death agonies were heard or seen by at least thirty-eight different people living in the apartment buildings surrounding the crime scene, and none of them called the police or tried to help her.

These witnesses, these neighbors, these fellow human beings later explained their lack of action to the police by saying: "It was none of my business;" "So many, many [other] times in the night I heard screams;" "I'm not the police;" "I couldn't make out what she said;" "I just saw the guy kneeling over her;" "I thought it was some kids having fun;" "I thought there must have been thirty calls already;" "Frankly, we were afraid." And the saddest one of all: "I was tired."

Jeff Pearlman, a Chicago *Tribune* reporter recently wrote, "Four decades after her death, Kitty Genovese is remembered not so much as a human being but as a cultural catch phrase for inexcusable indifference. The term *The Genovese Syndrome* has now become synonymous with the dark side of urban existence. Too often, we are too frightened, too alienated, too self absorbed to get involved in helping a human being in dire trouble."[13]

The allied notions of the narcissistic personality type, the "inability to forget about ourselves on purpose," the delimited perspective of the fortress of self, and the cool moral detachment of the bystander, results in a completely myopic view of reality which reduces all moral calculations to the overly simplistic—me, myself, and I. And this "sycophantic syndrome of self," as I call it, is most commonly and pervasively found where we work, in what we do to earn a living, and our ethical perspective on the purpose of business.

VII

A Philosophy of Work

Morality requires that businesses offer meaningful work because morality requires that all individuals have a right to a meaningful life.

Joanna B. Ciulla

Moral courage does not operate in a vacuum. In fact, it requires a social setting to be meaningful. In our contemporary society, we have made a fetish out of being ambitious and achieving financial success. Competition and rugged individualism are part of our collective myth and mantra. Looking out for one's own best interest has become a way of life, even though it regularly means that others get stepped on in the process. The notion that such behavior might be destructive to others as well as debasing to ourselves is rarely raised, let alone seriously considered. We live in a nation in which ethical *laissez-faire* has been elevated to a national credo. As a consequence, it has become terribly easy to lose our way. And the only time we have to apologize for our misdeeds or the misfortune we cause others is if we get caught (see Enron, Bernie Madoff, AIG, BP, and the entire cast of *Wall Street* and *Wall Street 2*).

I think that too many of us believe that the stakes and standards involved in modern economic activity are simply different from, more important than, or perhaps even antithetical to the principles and practices of ethics. Ethics is something we may preach and practice at home in our private lives, but not in business. After all, it would cost us prestige, position, profits, and success. Just as it is difficult in our personal lives to keep our narcissism in check, the task is made much more difficult in our work when cash, comfort, and sinecure are on the line.

Given the centrality of work in our lives—the sheer number of hours we put into the job, the money we make, the stuff it allows us to acquire, the kinds of status and success we can achieve on the job—how can work not affect our values and sense of ethics? How is it possible to retain a private sense of objectivity, impartiality, and a respectful concern for others? How is it possible to not be co-opted by the needs and demands of the workplace? How is it possible not to be at least swayed, if not totally compromised, by the work environment that sustains us?

Work, all work, creates its own self-contained moral universe. Every job, good or bad, creates its own experiences, its own standards, its own pace, and its own self-defined *weltanschauung* (worldview). Every job, depending on the intensity, depth, and duration of the individual worker's involvement, can have either immediate or long-term effects on the worker. The habits we acquire on the job, what we are exposed to, what is demanded of us, and the pressure of peers can change, influence, and/or erode our personal conduct and standards. At the very least: When everybody else in the workplace is doing "it" (whatever "it" is), isn't it natural to at least ask ourselves, "Why not me, too?"

The two individuals who have most eloquently explained the phenomenon of the institutional co-option of the individual worker on the job are Howard S. Schwartz and Robert Jackall. Schwartz, in *Narcissistic Process and Corporate Decay*, argues that corporations and businesses are not bastions of benign, community-orientated ethical reasoning, nor can they, because of the demands and requirements of business, be models of moral behavior.[1] The rule of business, says Schwartz, remains the survival of the fittest, and the goal of survival engenders a combative "us against them" mentality, which condones getting ahead by any means necessary. Schwartz calls this phenomenon "organizational totalitarianism." Organizations and the people who manage them create a self-contained, self-serving worldview, which rationalizes anything done on their behalf and which does not require justification on any grounds outside of themselves.[2]

This narcissistic perspective, Schwartz suggests, imposes Draconian requirements on all participants in organizational life: Do your work; achieve organizational goals; obey and exhibit loyalty to your superiors; disregard personal values and beliefs; obey the law when necessary, obfuscate it when possible; and deny internal or external information at odds with the stated organizational worldview. Within such a "totalitarian" logic, neither leaders nor followers operate as independent agents. To maintain their place or to get ahead, all must conform.

According to Robert Jackall, in *Moral Mazes*, organizations are examples of "patrimonial bureaucracies" wherein "fealty relations of personal loyalty" are the rule of organizational life.[3] Jackall argues that all corporations are like fiefdoms of the Middle Ages: The lord of the manor (CEO or president) offers protection, prestige, and status to his vassals (managers) and serfs (workers) in return for homage (commitment) and service (work). In such a system, says Jackall, advancement and promotion are predicated on loyalty, trust, politics, and personality at least as much as on experience, education, ability, and accomplishments. The central concern of the worker minion is to be known as a "can-do" employee, a "team player," "being at the right place at the right time," and "master of all the social rules." That's why in the corporate world, says Jackall, a thousand "attaboys" are wiped away with one "oh shit!"[4]

Jackall contends that the logic of every organization and the collective personality of the workplace conspire to override the desires and aspirations of the individual worker. No matter what a person believes off the job, on the job all of us are required to some extent to suspend, bracket, or only selectively manifest our personal convictions. "What is right in the corporation is not what is right in a person's home or his church. What is right in the corporation is what the guy above you wants from you."[5]

In Jackall's analysis, the primary imperative of every organization is to succeed. This goal of performance, which he refers to as "institutional logic," leads to the creation of a private moral universe that, by definition, is self-sustained, self-defined, and self-centered. Within such an environment, truth is socially defined, and moral behavior is determined solely by organizational needs. The key virtues, for all, become the virtues of the organization: goal preoccupation, problem solving, survival or success, and, most important, playing by the "house rules." In time, says Jackall, those initiated and invested in the system come to believe that they live in a self-contained world that is above outside critique and evaluation. As sociologist Kathleen McCourt has suggested:

> *It is difficult to be a good person in a society that is itself not good. People, after all, live and learn through the institutions of society—family, school, church, community, and the workplace—and these institutions must support the positive development of individuals if society is to produce succeeding generations of positive individuals.*[6]

To the catholic philosopher, humans are not herd animals but communal creatures. We are dependent on each other to survive and thrive. Whether we are good people or bad people as individuals, our collective existence requires us to continually make choices about "what we ought to do" in regard to others. Like it or not, then, we are by definition moral creatures. Ethics is primarily a communal, collective enterprise, not a solitary one. It is the study of our web of relationships with others. As a communal exercise, ethics is the attempt to work out the rights and obligations we have and share with others. Defining ethics is not difficult, but living ethically is. Why? Because ethics requires us to be concerned about the rights and wellbeing of others. It requires us to stop thinking of ourselves as the sole center of the universe. It requires us to transcend the simplistic equation of "me, myself, and I." It requires us to be just, reasonable, and objective. It requires us to do something we do not always want to do: be our rational selves in regard to others. It requires us to have the moral courage to live out what we value, what we hold dear, what we believe in.

⟿

No one is neutral about the topic of work. Everyone has an opinion. The reason is simple. For 95% of us, work is an entirely non-discretionary matter. Most of us must work. As adults there is nothing that more preoccupies our lives. From the approximate ages of twenty-one to seventy we spend our lives working. We do not sleep as much as we work, spend time with our families as much as we work, eat or recreate or rest as much as we work. Whether we love our work or hate it, succeed in it or fail, achieve fame or infamy through it, we are all—like Sisyphus—condemned to push and chase that thing we call our *job*, our *career*, our *occupation*, even our *calling* or *vocation* all our days. "Even those of us who desperately don't want to work," said Ogden Nash, "must work in order to earn enough money so that they won't have to work anymore."

I have always been fascinated by work. As a boy, I marveled at the long hours of hard labor put in by my father, grandfathers, and uncles. I was equally impressed with the skills and efforts of my mother, grandmothers, and assorted aunts in maintaining comfortable and efficient homes while also being forced to hold down full- or part-time jobs.

I come from a family of workers who immigrated to the United States in the early 1900s and who, by dint of their labor, not only survived but thrived. My family valued and honored work. They believed in it and praised it. It was their yardstick for measuring status and success. Work was an obligation of adult life, although there was no shame in being "out of work" because you lost your job due to economic hard times. The only sin was in not wanting to work, in being lazy.

My maternal grandfather, for example, was finally forced out of his janitorial job for insurance reasons when he was in his late eighties. My father and uncle stayed on their jobs well into their seventies. My beloved godmother worked for the same company for forty-eight years. And my mother retired in her late sixties, only because I begged her to do so in order to help care for my youngest child. For the men and women of my family, work was the active demonstration of their love and the proof of their commitment to one another. Work was a source of pride and a badge of honor for responsibilities accepted and borne bravely.

In an old, Italian neighborhood of Chicago, long before the cloistering effects of television and air-conditioning, summer nights were spent outside. While it was still light, the boys played baseball in the street, the girls jumped rope on the sidewalk, and the adults—segregated by gender—would sit on the front steps and talk. When it got too dark to play, the younger children were sent to bed. The older kids had the option of laying claim to a porch of their own or joining the adults, but only to listen, never to be heard. More often than not, I joined the adults, sometimes the women but most often the men.

The women talked about everything. They talked about work, but usually about the personalities in their workplaces rather than the specifics of their jobs. They also talked about department store sales, the rising price of coffee at the A&P, what they had made for dinner, who was pregnant, who was sick, who had died, and who was about to get married. They were alternately silly and serious, and there was no limit to the range of topics they would discuss over an evening. As a budding guy, I wasn't all that interested in most of the "girl talk."

The men's conversation, on the other hand, was limited almost completely to two topics and two topics only: sports and work. Since most of the men were either recently arrived or first-generation citizens, the sports conversation didn't last very long. The only game they even vaguely understood was baseball, and the only players they cared about were those of Italian descent—especially Joe (Giuseppe Paolo) DiMaggio, the Yankee Clipper. So, what they ended up talking about all night, *every night*, was their work. They bemoaned it, complained about it, dissected and decried it. They also bragged and boasted about their work and retold complicated stories extolling their efforts, duties, and responsibilities on the job. Work was the center of their lives, and—love it or hate it—work was the only thing these guys really knew and understood well enough to discuss at length.

I was both fascinated and frightened by what these men had to say. They taught me that there was dignity in work, a sense of fulfillment and satisfaction in earning your own way and providing for your family. They taught me that an honest man should never be too proud to do whatever was necessary—no matter how humbling or backbreaking the effort—in order to earn an honest dollar. They also taught me that work could wear you out and break you down.

These men knew that although working was a human necessity, not every job offered satisfaction, meaning, or even decent money. The honor was in surviving the doing, not in what was being done. Having to do unpleasant, unsatisfying work could never be used as an excuse for not working at all. They taught me—as Abraham Lincoln's father taught him—to work hard but not necessarily to love my work. At the same time, they warned me in no uncertain terms not to do the kind of work they had to do to earn a living. They told me to go to school, get an education, find better work—work that did not break your spirit or your back, work that did not leave you empty and disappointed.

As I grew up I quickly realized that the lessons and wisdom of my neighbors and family were not unique to the Italian-American community. The "work ethic," whether it was "Protestant," "Catholic," "immigrant," or anything else, was the law of the land. Work was as expected as the sun rising each day. Ironically, one needed only to consult the wording of death notices in the newspapers to fully appreciate the importance of work in our lives at the time. Obituaries almost always list the occupation of the deceased first, the relationships last: "Joseph Doe, leading public interest lawyer, dead at seventy-two…. He is survived by his wife, Jane, and his beloved children…."[7] As Gandhi purportedly suggested (in language that predates the dawn of political correctness): "A man is the sum of his actions, of what he has done, of what he can do. Nothing else."

Work is not just about earning a livelihood, about getting paid, about gainful employment. Nor is it only about the use of one's mind and body to accomplish a specific task or project. Work is also one of the most significant contributing factors to one's inner life and development. Beyond mere survival, we create ourselves in our work. In his classic article, "Work and Self," Everett C. Hughes argues that work is fundamental to the development of personality. Because work preoccupies our lives and is the central focus of our time and energies, it not only provides us with an income, it literally names us, identifies us—both to ourselves and to others. Hughes was convinced that even when we are dissatisfied with or dislike the work we do, choice of occupation irrevocably "labels" us, and that we cannot understand a person unless we understand his or her work and how he or she deals with it.[8]

In the long run, work can prove to be a boon or a burden, creative or crippling, a means to personal happiness or a prescription for despair. But no matter where we might wind up on this spectrum, *where* we work, *how* we work, *what we do* at work, and the general *climate* and *culture* of our particular workplace indelibly mark us for life. Work is the means by which we form our character and complete ourselves as persons. We literally create ourselves in our work. To restate the old Italian proverb *"Tu sei quello che mangi"* ("You are what you eat"), in regard to work: *"Tu sei quello che fai"* ("You are the work you do"). Work is a necessary and defining activity in the development of the adult personality.

According to Catholic theologian Gregory Baum, "Labor is the axis of human self-making."[9] We both establish and recognize ourselves in our work. Work allows us to find out what we can and cannot do, how we are seen by others, and how we see ourselves. Through work we discover our boundaries and limits as well as our capacities for success. Work is the yardstick by which we measure ourselves against others. It is the means by which we establish our rank, role, and function within a community. Work not only conditions our lives; it is the necessary condition for life.

Assuredly other factors enter into the question of self-identity: for example, genetic inheritance, race, gender, ethnicity, sexual orientation, religious training, and family background. But even with all of these, work remains an irreducible given, the most common experience of adult life. The lessons we learn at work help formulate who we become and what we value as individuals and as a society. Whatever the conditions of our labor, work shapes us and, unfortunately, often malforms us. But, for good or ill, work makes us human, because we all make something of ourselves through work, and in so doing we recognize ourselves and others in the task of working.[10]

A number of years ago, I attended a family wedding, and the first person I saw was my Uncle Frank. "Hey, college kid," he said to me as he shook my hand in a vice-like grip and peppered my shoulder with a series of heavy blows. "How you been?" Uncle Frank was in his late-seventies, but his punches still hurt, as did his annoying habit of calling me "college kid." I had just turned fifty-five.

"Uncle Frank," I said, massaging my shoulder, "you look great. Where did you get that tan? Have you been playing a lot of golf?"

"Naw," he said, "you know I hate golf. I had a couple of jobs this month."

"Jobs? But you've been retired for ten years!"

"Yeah, but they were easy jobs," said Uncle Frank. "A couple of driveways, some concrete steps, a few sidewalks. It was a piece of cake."

"Uncle Frank," I said, "this doesn't make sense. Is something wrong? Do you need money?"

"No! No!" he said. "It's nothing like that."

"Then why?" I persisted. "Why did you take these jobs?"

Uncle Frank smiled, grabbed me roughly and drew me to him. "Because," he said with a wink, "I wanted to see if I could still do it, college kid. *Capice*? I just wanted to see if I could still do it."

When I finally got to my life's work as a writer and a teacher, I discovered a rich legacy and tradition in Catholic social teaching on the nature of work and the rights of the worker that closely mirrors the lessons I absorbed as a young boy on various porch steps of my old neighborhood. Although the magisterium of the Church has always been concerned about individual rights, social justice, and the care of the poor, there are two important papal documents that make crucial pronouncement regarding the "rights of workers" and the "role of work in regard to the development and identity of individual workers": Pope Leo XIII's 1891 encyclical letter, *The Condition of Labor (Rerum Novarum)*; and Pope John Paul II's 1981 publication *On Human Work (Laborem Exercens)*.

Although historically work has been seen primarily as a necessity or a duty—in all the many meanings of the terms—both *The Condition of Labor* and *On Human Work* are an attempt to recast our conventional thinking about work. Both encyclicals contend that although work may be part of humanity's banishment and punishment, it is also part of a person's definition, salvation, and mission in the world.

Leo XIII's meaning is clear: "So far as bodily labor is concerned, [humans] even before the Fall [were] not destined to be wholly idle; and certainly what [their] will at the time would have freely embraced to [their] soul's delight, necessity afterwards forced [them] to accept, with a feeling of irksomeness, for the expiation of [their] guilt."[11] The implication here, and the tone of the entire encyclical, is that although the toil of labor may be part of our "curse," work is also a natural part of our destiny and character.

John Paul II is much more explicit in his claims:

The Church finds in the very first pages of the Book of Genesis the source of her conviction that work is a fundamental dimension of human existence on earth. An analysis of these texts makes us aware that they express—sometimes in an archaic way of manifesting thought— the fundamental truths about the human person in the context of the mystery of creation itself.[12]

The passages the pope is referring to and the ones he harkens back to again and again in the encyclical are from Genesis:[13]

Then God said, "Let us make humankind in our image, according to our likeness; and let them have dominion over the fish of the sea, and over the birds of the air, and over the cattle, and over all the wild animals of the earth, and over every creeping thing that creeps upon the earth." So God created humankind in his image, in the image of God he created them; male and female he created them. God blessed them, and God said to them, "Be fruitful and multiply, and fill the earth and subdue it; and have dominion over the fish of the sea and over the birds of the air and over every living thing that moves upon the earth."[14]

In selecting these Scripture passages, John Paul II was arguing that God first created the human person in his image as creator/worker and gave us what he called the "work bench" of the world from which to wrestle and fashion a meaningful life. The gift of life and the power of creation are prior to humankind's exile from Eden. Moreover, he claims that:

God's fundamental and original intention with regard to [humans]… was not withdrawn or canceled out even when [they], having broken the original covenant with God, heard the words: In the sweat of your face you shall eat bread. These words refer to the sometimes heavy toil that from then onward has accompanied human work; but they do not alter the fact that work is the means whereby [people] achieve that "domination" which is proper to [them] over the visible world by "subjecting" the earth.[15]

For John Paul II, people must work because God has commanded it and because God's original creative act defined the person as a worker.[16] The central message of *On Human Work* is that work is a positive force in people's lives and not simply a burden to be tolerated and endured. Work is the divinely endowed mechanism by which humankind fulfills itself and establishes its stewardship over the world.[17] In other words, work is the agency by which humanity completes itself and transforms the world. Therefore, since people are created for work and defined by work, work is "a fundamental right of all human beings."[18] Or, in the words of Pope Paul VI in *On Promoting the Development of Peoples (Populorum Progressio)*, insofar as humans are created in the image and likeness of God, they have the "right to get from [the earth] what is necessary."[19]

Harry Braverman, a Marxist labor historian, has stated that all forms of life strive to sustain themselves. Plants absorb moisture and sunlight; animals feed on plant life or prey on other animals. But the activity of animals to procure food and protection is not, strictly speaking, work. Work, said Braverman, is an activity that intentionally alters the materials of nature to improve on their usefulness.[20] Like Braverman, John Paul II asserts in the prefatory paragraph to his encyclical that only humans are capable of work, and only humans, of all the species, work, because only they possess reason and freedom and by their design are capable of creating the conditions necessary for survival, growth, and development.[21]

Only humans work—but however true it may be that we are "destined to work" and "called to work," what must always be kept in clear perspective is that work is for us and we are not for work.[22] "Just as all human activity," said John Paul II, quoting the Second Vatican Council, "proceeds from [human beings], so too it must all be ordered toward [human beings]."[23] The human person, not the products or "economic advantage(s)" of his or her labor, is the "proper subject of work."[24]

For John Paul II, then, what happens to the "subject of work" at work is more important than what the work itself produces. The true function of work for the person is derived not from the "object achieved," but from one's "actual engagement" in the process of production; that is, from the labor of one's hands and mind. The fundamental error of the history of economic theory, says John Paul II, is that it has almost always considered "human labor solely according to its economic purpose."[25] But the "gospel of work" he wishes to advance claims that "the value of human work is not primarily the kind of work being done, but the fact that the one who is doing it is a person." The sources of the dignity of work, he claims, "are to be sought primarily in the subjective dimension [of work], not in…[its] objective use."[26]

Another fundamental error of economic history, said John Paul II, has been the contention that the means and instruments of production—that is, capital—is prior to and more important than the labor of those who are part of the production process. For John Paul II, although labor and capital are in some sense "inseparable,"[27] labor is ontologically distinct from and prior to capital, because all capital is the result of human work.[28] *On Human Work* maintains that "the wealth of nations originates from no other source than the labor of workers."[29] But unlike Leo XIII, John Paul II does not accept that they are "equally balanced counterparts"[30] and therefore have equal priority. For John Paul II, if the person has priority over things and if man is the subject of work and the efficient cause of the production process,[31] then capital—that whole collection of instruments and things necessary for and used in production—must be subordinate to the labor that allows the capital to produce wealth.[32]

Work, says John Paul II, is the means by which we create ourselves and become "more a human being."[33] Work is that which forms us, gives us a focus, provides us a vehicle for personal expression, and offers us a means for personal definition. Work makes us human precisely because we make something of ourselves through our work. We need work in order to finish and define our natures. Just as the world is not a fixed thing but needs to be developed and changed, so too is the human soul. Both are continuously being produced by human labor.

We are by nature, as Aristotle said, social creatures; we are also by nature, according to Leo XIII and John Paul II, productive creatures. Work is about human living, human being, human becoming. Work is the direct expression of our unique human excellence, and the direct expression of the way we establish ourselves in the world.[34] A person's life is built up every day from work, and from work humankind derives its specific dignity and worth.[35] Both popes argue that we need work; we are formed by work; and the quality of our lives is directly dependent on the quality of the work we do. Moreover, to be denied work is to be denied far more than the things that work can buy. It is to be denied a basic and primary organizing principle in life; it is to be denied the ability to define and respect ourselves as persons.

∼

Novelist and film director Elia Kazan said that the one absolute lesson he has learned in life is that our careers and our identities are inextricably bound up. Indeed they are equivalent. People are what they do, and what people do affects every aspect of who they are. For good or ill, we are known and know ourselves by the work we do. The meter and measure of work serves as our mapping device to explain and order the geography of our lives. Our work circumscribes what we know and how we select and categorize the things we choose to notice and hold important. The lessons we learn in our work and at our workplaces become the metaphors we apply to our own life and the lives of others. It is the means by which we digest the world. As Samuel Butler said: "Every man's work, whether it be literature or music or pictures or architecture or anything else, is always a portrait of himself."

In the end Descartes is wrong! It isn't *"Cogito, ergo sum."* ("I think, therefore I am.") It's *"Laboro, ergo sum."* ("I work, therefore I am.") Work is not something detached from the rest of human life. It rather is synonymous with life. In the words of another pope, Pius XI in 1931, we humans are "born to labor, as a bird is born to fly."[36]

VIII

THE PHILOSOPHY OF LAUGHTER AND LEISURE

For lack of attention
a thousand forms of loveliness
elude us every day.

Evelyn Underhill

The history of humor is long and convoluted. The oldest recorded joke dates back to Greece in the fourth or fifth century A.D. It can be found in a book of 264 jokes called the *Philogelus* or the *Laughter-Lover*. ("'How shall I cut your hair?' a talkative barber asked a customer. 'In silence,' says the customer.") In Augustus' Rome, a writer by the name of Melissus is said to have compiled approximately 150 joke anthologies. During the Renaissance, papal secretary Poggio Bracciolini put together a bestselling collection of 273 jokes, puns, and humorous anecdotes about obesity, flatulence, and the ever-popular clerical sexual promiscuity and drunkenness. In Shakespeare's time, jest books, primarily made up of artless scatology, were all the rage.[1] And, during the Civil War, Abraham Lincoln was able to find moments of diversion and laughter by reading bestselling satirist and storytellers Charles Farrar Browne, David Locke, and Robert H. Newell.[2]

According to psychologist Robert Provine, laughter is part and parcel of our genetic makeup. But exactly why we laugh, what makes us laugh, and the ultimate purpose of laughter is open to multiple interpretations.[3] Laughter can be a response to many things. We laugh when we are frightened, shocked, or scared. We often laugh when we are amazed or surprised. We laugh when we are amused, delighted, or charmed. And, in social settings, most commonly we laugh at stories and jokes. The laughter of joke telling is a way we can create shared experiences, common frames of reference, and a sense of community. Jokes can be an attempt to reach out and commiserate with others. They can change the mood and the tone of an otherwise awkward or unpleasant situation. They can be gifts that we offer others for the purpose of establishing friendships.[4] As comedian Victor Borge succinctly put it: "Laughter is the shortest distance between two people."[5]

Metaphysically speaking, perhaps the most important attribute of laughter and joke telling is that humor can act as both a sword and a shield to defend ourselves against overwhelming issues in life. According to University of Chicago epistemologist and erstwhile stand-up comic, Ted Cohen, jokes can detox the perennial, unsolvable, intolerable, and unavoidable problems of life. To joke about illness, death, God, sex, aging and other no-no topics is a way of defanging or domesticating something that essentially cannot be tamed. It is a way, says Cohen, of being in charge of something that we really cannot control. Joking about something deep or dangerous is a way of talking about it, examining it in a way that doesn't scare us, numb us, and rob us of our joy for life. Jokes allow us to dwell on the incomprehensible without dying from fear or going mad. Laughter and joke-telling are a way to speak of the unspeakable. Humor gives us the courage to endure that which we cannot understand or avoid.[6] It even gives us permission to wax philosophical about life without taking ourselves too seriously.

Friedrich Nietzsche has suggested that to gaze too long into the "gaping abyss"[7] leads to despair and futility. I want to argue that humor, laughter, and joking are a way to gaze into the abyss, confront the unknowable and unanswerable, and perhaps find comfort and perspective even if no absolute answers are to be found. Humor can offer alternative insights and perspective, grant some relief from our existential crises and fears, and help us bear the unbearable and deal with the insoluble. Humor allows us to gaze into the abyss and not be defeated.[8]

∼

The essence of humor is the ability to laugh both *with* and *at* life. It is the ability to appreciate the whimsical, the comical, the silly, as well as the absolutely ludicrous and absurdly incongruous aspects of existence. It is the ability to step back and be amused, delighted, or surprised by whatever happens.

Humor prevents us from perceiving reality as a personal attack or a personal affront. Humor is about our ability to transcend self, to celebrate our collective experience and essential sameness. Humor allows us to laugh at our personal and collective vulnerability. The humorless person is too self-absorbed, too aggressively self-centered, too myopic to see beyond the needs, wants, and desires of self. Humor has to do with transcending the ambivalence, absurdity, despair, fragility, narcissism, and nonsense of life.[9]

French philosopher André Comte-Sponville suggests that humor is a kind of mourning and mocking of the human condition. "(Humor) accepts the human condition as sad—scary, and then talks about it, pokes fun at it, laughs at it, and laughs at our feeble response to it. In so doing, it frees us from dread. It softens the blow of reality."[10] Perhaps Nietzsche captured it best: "I know…why it is man alone who laughs—he alone suffers so deeply that he had to invent laughter."[11] At bottom, "humor is a form of *joyful disillusionment*"; that is, humor allows us to endure without false illusion or fear the paradoxes and perils of life.[12]

The study of philosophy is, of course, another way to address the perennial and unavoidable problems of life. William James muses that philosophy is an attempt to make sense out of the "booming, buzzing, confusion of reality." However, there are no guarantees. Although philosophers are lovers (*philo*) of wisdom (*sophia*), that does not mean that there is necessarily any wisdom to be found or that philosophers will necessarily be able to find whatever wisdom is there. Although philosophy and the telling of jokes do not share the same pedigree, in regard to many of the inescapable and impenetrable questions in life, both have an allied heuristic function and purpose. Philosophy, like joke-telling, can help us to organize, interpret, and possibly understand or at least face and confront the fundamental issues of existence.

Of course, religion—like philosophy—is ripe for humor. For example:

A man arrives at the gates of heaven. St. Peter asks, "Religion?"

The man says "Methodist." St. Peter looks down his list, and says, "Go to room twenty-eight, but be very quiet as you pass room eight."

Another man arrives at the gates of heaven. "Religion?"

"Baptist"

"Go to room eighteen, but be very quiet as you pass room eight."

A third man arrives at the gates. "Religion?"

"Presbyterian."

"Go to room eleven, but be very quiet as you pass room eight."

The man says, "I can understand there being different rooms for different religions, even different Christian denominations, but why must I be quiet when I pass room eight?"

St. Peter says, "The Catholics are in room eight, and they think they're the only ones here."[13]

I am deadly earnest about arriving at truth through joke-telling. Humor, philosophy, and religion all ask us to look at the world from a different perspective. They force us out of our usual, more comfortable, safe perspectives on reality and, in the process, jar us out of "our dogmatic slumber" (in the words of Immanuel Kant, who was not a very funny guy).

Joking and laughter play a vital role in life. We need to laugh at both the little and the big issues in order to find balance and moments of peace. Of course, there is a caveat: Humor is not a cure for life…but it can be a helpful anesthesia! I am convinced that laughter reinforces our humanity, encourages hope, and allows us to endure with dignity. Both seriousness and silliness are critical parts of a meaningful life.

Laughter, of course, is a subset (as they say in Logic) of the bigger subset of leisure, which is the activity of slowing down and being reflective, joyous, playful, and thoughtful about life. The statistics are clear. Whether we want to or not, most of us work too much. Don't get me wrong, work is important. Our work gives access to salary, stuff, success, and sense of identity. But, just as we all need to work and fulfill ourselves, we also need to play.

The word *play*, from the Middle English term *plega*, "to leap for joy, to dance, to rejoice, to be glad," is about activity outside the sphere of the customary, the necessary, or the materially useful. According to the poet Diane Ackerman, play "is a refuge from ordinary life, a sanctuary of the mind, where one is exempt from life's customs, methods, and decrees."[14] Fellow poet Donald Hall suggests that play is about "absorbedness"—"a noun with a lot of verb in it"—which connotes concentration, contentment, loss of self, loss of time, happiness, and joy.[15]

For both children and adults, play is about awe, wonder, rapture, and enthusiasm. Play is something we want to do, something we choose to do that is not work, is enjoyable, and gives us gratification and fun. In play, we drop inhibitions, gives us permission to imagine, to be creative, to be curious. Play, like laughter, is an end in itself, something done without any other incentive except for the pleasure involved in the activity.[16]

In a cover story in the *Utne Reader*, Mark Harris argues that children are masters of play. They need to play. It's what they do. It's the way they ingest the world. It's the way they learn. By acting out or playing out a situation, they acquire cognitive and motor skills. In play, they create a map of reality and come to know and define the other players in the game. Play, says the psychiatrist Lenore Terr, is not frivolous. It is one of the ways we become human. Play, like laughter, say Terr, is crucial at every stage of life. Play, for both children and adults alike, helps us unlock the door to the world of ourselves.[17] According to Stuart Brown, president of the National Institute of Play, play is part of the "developmental sequences of becoming a human primate. If you look at what produces learning and memory and well-being, play is as fundamental as any other aspect of life, including sleep and dreams."[18]

All of us need more play. All of us need to "vacate" ourselves from our jobs and the wear and tear of the "everydayness" of our lives. All of us need to get absorbed in and focused on something of interest outside of ourselves—to escape, if only for a while, in order to retain our perspective on *who we are* and *who we don't want to be*.

True play, as found in many sports, represents a kind of freedom of expression, a chance for openness and creativity. Play is a way of doing something and nothing at the same time. It's a way of both letting go and losing yourself without getting totally lost in the process. It's a way of experimenting with reality. It's an excuse to laugh, a catalyst for growth, a way of finding balance. Without play, we risk the diminishment of self.

Like all forms of play, sports are something we can do or view "for the love of it," "for its own sake alone," "for the joy of the doing." At their best, sports offer a benign distraction, simple entertainment, an escape or buffer against the realities of the everyday world. In the words of the philosopher Baruch Spinoza: "Give men an open field, a ball to catch or kick, or something or someone to chase, and they are happy, despite all else."[19]

But besides being fun, sports are supposed to be challenging, expansive, expressive, and growthful. Plato, in his classic works *The Republic* and *The Laws*, argues that the purpose of all individual and team sports is to teach *completion*, *coordination*, and *cooperation*.

Completion: The use and testing of one's body.
To extend, expand one's range of physical abilities.
To learn the limits of one's endurance and abilities.
To learn to be comfortable in one's body.

Coordination: To synchronize body and mind.
To anticipate.
To image, to visualize.
To plan, to strategize.

Cooperation: Community effort.
Collective behavior.
Team work.

There is, of course, one more "C" word to consider, *competition*. The concepts of *completion*, *coordination*, *cooperation*, and *competition* in sports are, I think, intimately connected. The Latin word for competition is *competere*, "to seek together" (not "to beat" the other). The cliché, "There is no I in TEAM," is wrong. Or at best it's only literally true. There is an "I" in TEAM; in fact, there are many "I's." The trick is to learn how to blend the energy, initiative, and ability of the various "I's" involved in the pursuit of the same goal.

For Plato, all children, girls and boys alike, must participate in sports. Sports, he argued, are a necessary ingredient in the formation of both the individual person and the collective community. The concepts of self, citizen, and sports participation were, for Plato, conjoined. This is exactly why General Douglas MacArthur, when he was commandant of West Point, required all cadets to participate in a team sport. As a student of history, MacArthur was convinced it was on the playing fields of England that the British officer class learned the lessons of *completion*, *coordination*, and *cooperation* that ultimately enabled them to defeat Napoleon at Waterloo.[20]

Golf is a sport, a game, which can be played in groups (foursomes), in teams (Ryder Cup Competition), or alone (a phenomenon which, for financial reasons, is more and more frowned upon by golf course owners). In fact, it can be argued that golf—like running, swimming, skiing, and skating—is one of those sports where you are basically competing against yourself even when you are playing with others. For many purists (some people refer to them as "fans," from the Latin *fanaticus*, fanatic), golf is the ultimate solitary sport because the outcome, no matter what the external variables (course condition, weather), is entirely dependent on the skill of the individual player. So, in essence, each player's chief rivals are his or her best and worst rounds of golf. For the true purist, golf is a John Wayne thing. It's about "true grit," "determination," and "dedication." It's about "commitment," "overcoming mistakes," and "never giving up." It's about "rugged individualism."

My father discovered golf in the Eisenhower administration, and his life and the life of our family changed forever. Golf was like some "non-chemical hallucinogen,"[21] and he was immediately addicted. From the beginning, it was always a "game." That is, it was always about "play." It was about the "pleasure and the joy" of the doing. But, for him and for so many others, it was also much more. It became his avocation, his passion, his *raison d'etre*. Anytime my father was not at work, not involved with a project around the home or with the family, he was either playing golf or somehow working on his golf game.

To begin with, my father subscribed to every golf magazine. He read and reread each of them from cover to cover. He would save articles and carefully file them away in two overstuffed filing cabinets he kept in his "golf room" in the basement. He would cut out action shots of famous players and pin them on the wall by his "golf desk." He would often sit for hours listening to golfing records and tapes while staring at the photos. And then, there were the books. He bought every book he could find on the subject. Instructional books, novels, picture books, short stories, it didn't matter. If it was about golf, he bought it. As golf columnist Timothy J. Carroll has pointed out, books give hope to every committed golfer's eternal quest for the "perfect swing" and the "perfect game."[22]

Then there was the equipment. Although proper dress and fashion have always been part of the game, this was the one facet of the game where my father went his own way. As far as he was concerned, most golfers worried too much about clothes and the right look. He was convinced that excess concern about one's wardrobe was an affectation as well as a distraction. As far as Dad was concerned, khakis or cut-offs were perfect, as long as you were wearing a decent pair of shoes. For him, the game came down to the quality of your clubs. He was especially fascinated with putters and, at one point, he owned over forty of them. He was also in love with his woods. He collected woods, both for their beauty and their driving power. He waxed every one of them regularly, and every year he had a few of his favorite clubs professionally sanded, stained, and varnished. I vividly remember the first time he used a titanium "wood." After hitting half a bucket of balls, he sat next to me with tears in his eyes. "God," he said, "I wish I had this club thirty years ago when I could have done something with it. I could have improved my game by four or five strokes. This just isn't fair!"

From mid-May until late-October, come rain or shine, my father, for over fifty years, played golf at least twice a week, and at least once a week he went to a "Stop and Sock" to hit three buckets of practice balls. During the winter, he often worked seven days a week, but during the golfing season, he took off every Wednesday and Sunday. On Sundays, he played thirty-six holes of golf with three other men. But Wednesdays were my father's high holy days. On Wednesdays, he regularly golfed thirty-six holes, sometimes fifty-four holes, and, on occasion, seventy-two holes on foot, by himself.

For my father, this was golf at its finest. It was all about him and his talents against the game itself. He kept every scorecard, filed them by date, and compared his scores from week to week and from year to year. What he was after was not just his best score, but his best form and strategy. For my dad, the "how" was just as important as the "count." He was as concerned about what the Italians might call *bella figura*—good form, good figure, good technique—as he was about the final score. For my dad, making a great shot by accident meant you actually missed the shot you intended to make.

For all of my father's, shall we say, excessive exuberance about golf, and despite his obsessions with details and fanaticism about form, Dad loved golf as a game. For him, golf was something of beauty and wonder in itself, and playing it gave him a sense of childish joy. He was not a happy man by nature, nor given to deep philosophical thought. But when he picked up a club and addressed the ball, he was, at least at times, poetry in motion. He was taken out of himself. He was lost in the joy of the act. In the words of Thomas á Kempis, "in losing himself, he found himself," at least for the moment. Golf was my father's Zen, his "refuge from ordinary life," and his way to pursue "happiness and joy."

For the average golfer, golf is a hobby, a social event, a bit of sun, a little exercise. But for my father, and I venture to guess hundreds of thousands of other people who play this "ridiculously hard game" (at least according to Tiger Woods, who has finally found out just how hard it is), it teaches humility, patience, self-confidence, as well as technique, timing, and touch. And it results in a sense of *completion*, *coordination*, and *cooperation* strong enough to satisfy even General MacArthur.

So I say, both philosophically and personally to all of these people smitten by the game—play on! To golf is to play! To golf is to be!

And finally—I can hear the sighs of relief from here—leisure doesn't just mean sitting around on our duffs doing no-thing. It means being open to and engaged in life. It means seeking new and different experiences whenever they are presented to us. For many of us, and certainly for me, that includes travel.

The Chinese philosopher Lin Yutang said that the true purpose of travel is not rest or recovery but rediscovery and renewal. In travel, he said, we "should become lost and unknown." He chides vacationers who bring with them handfuls of letters of introduction so they will become known wherever they are. Anonymity, he claims, is far better. To have no fixed hours, no inquisitive neighbors, no mail, no email messages, no cellphones or faxes, offers us a chance to expand our horizons and reevaluate and possibly redefine who we are. For Lin Yutang, vacations are opportunities to rediscover our basic humanness apart from our accustomed personas and roles in life.[23]

Safari is a Swahili word meaning "journey" or "to travel," but it has come to mean so very much more. Imbued with a sense of the exotic, the word has today become symbolic of something far more romantic. I didn't want to go to Africa because I had watched too many Tarzan of the Apes episodes or read too much Hemingway—although I had done both. I didn't want to go to hunt or even photograph the wildlife with a zoom-lens 35-mm camera. Nor did I want to go in order to sit around a campfire at night in my special-order safari jacket from Abercrombie and Finch. I wanted to go because I was afraid I would miss seeing the Serengeti before it turned into a "Busch Garden Petting Zoo." Or, worse yet, before there was nothing left to see. I wanted to go because I wanted to breathe and smell the air where our earliest ancestors stood up, looked around, and began to become human. I wanted to go because I was afraid I would miss seeing and experiencing the place that was the cradle of human life and existence. I wanted to return to my human roots where, relatively speaking, so few of us have been.

Africa may not be the seat of all of western civilization, but it is the site of the birth of humankind, and it is the repository of the fossil remains of our earliest ancestors. The African continent is now generally recognized as the main birthplace of the human group. Life did develop elsewhere, but Africa is where the spark was ignited and the flame persisted and spread.

Somewhere on the Serengeti and in the general area ranging from Mount Kilimanjaro to the Ngoro Ngoro Crater and Olduvai Gorge, our ancient ancestors began the long, slow process of becoming fully human. Somewhere in Central Africa, we came down out of the trees, stood up, looked around, and became who we are. However, as biped mammals, we are not exactly an overly impressive species. Short, slow, with no fur or protective covering, we are not particularly strong or powerful nor do we have large claws or teeth. But what makes us special directly contributed to our survival. We could think. We could choose. We could scheme. We wound up being at the top of the food chain because we could out-plot and out-plan our fellow predators.

∽

The flight time from Chicago to Tanzania was twenty-two hours with an eight-hour layover in Holland. It was nine at night and dark as stone when my wife and I landed. I couldn't see my hand in front of my face—let along Mt. Kilimanjaro towering above me. But I knew I was in Africa. I could smell it. Literally, I could almost taste it. It tasted green. Yes, green. The smell was almost primordial. It smelled like the "soup of life."

Tanzania is a country of savannahs, wide vistas, towering volcanoes and mountains, and eleven national parks and game reserves that constitute one-quarter of the country's land area. Its official language is English. Its national language is Swahili. And it accommodates one-hundred and twenty tribal languages as part of its heritage. To the outside world, perhaps the two most commonly known facts about Tanzania are questions and answers only to be found in the games *Trivial Pursuit* or *Jeopardy*: 1. (Q) Who said: "Dr. Livingston I presume?" (A) Henry Morgan Stanley. 2. (Q) Who hunted and camped at the base of Kilimanjaro and later wrote a short story about it that was made into a film staring Gregory Peck and Susan Hayward? (A) Ernest Hemingway—*The Snows of Kilimanjaro*.

We spent twelve days in the bush. It was never boring, always beautiful, and sometimes overwhelming in its sights and sounds. Each day was a gift. The bush, I quickly found out, is alive with sights and sounds around the clock. During the day, wildebeest honk their presence to one and all. Zebra snort and stomp to make themselves heard. Elephants trumpet to one another constantly. But it's at night that the real symphony begins. Between the cicada's piercing shrill, the throaty growl of the cheetahs, the snarling semi-laughter of the hyenas—the night is a cacophony of sounds and rhythms that both delighted and fascinated me.

On any given day as we drove through the bush in our Land Cruisers we saw: huge herds of cape buffalos; a journey of giraffes; thousands of wildebeest; a dazzle of zebras; gazelle and antelope of every size, shape, and color; large families of elephants—ranging from old bulls to teenagers; a cash of rhinos; a raft of hippopotami; large congresses of baboons; an occasional leap of leopards; and twenty-foot-long crocodiles that seem to be part of our prehistoric past. It never seemed to stop, and it never ceased to amaze me.

Sometimes, it's hard to see the face of God in our fellow humans. But stare an immense elephant, a plump hippo, a graceful impala, or a clumsy but cute flamingo in the eye. I for one saw—if not God's face—at least God's signature in the handiwork.

In Maaisi, the Serengeti means "endless plains." The Serengeti measures 5,500 square miles and is roughly the size of Connecticut. Its vastness is hard to comprehend even as you're experiencing it. We drove through it for hours on end and the horizon never seemed to change and its vastness felt undiminished. We were dwarfed by it. It was like driving through a sea of endless elephant grass. Its effect was hypnotic. You became lost in the moment. In real time it was June of 1999. But it could have been 1899 or 1399 or even 599 B.C. It was anytime, every time. As we drove on and on through the golden grass, I could not help but think: How did our ancestors survive on this ocean of a plain, naked, with little food or water, unable to outfight a lion or outrun a cheetah? How did we live long enough to reproduce? How did we buy enough time to develop our skills of reflection and reasoning?

I awoke on our last morning on the Serengeti—out of sorts, ill-at-ease, angry, and melancholic. I was missing Africa already. I had not expected to be so deeply touched. Africa, for me, was far more than an exotic, unusual destination. It was more than a vacation, or just something different to do. Africa was and is—a gift. It was a dream. An experience I won't and can't forget, or ever take for granted.

The very first line of Isak Dinesen's memoir *Out of Africa* reads: "I had a farm in Africa, at the foot of the Ngon Hills." If I were writing my memoirs now, perhaps my opening line would be: "I once had a safari in Africa, and nothing since has ever been the same." Happily, since that first safari, I have been able to go back nine more times. And each time, the magic is there again, just like the first time.

∼

Humor, leisure, travel, and play are essential parts of the human experience. They are not just childish pursuits. They are not just frivolous distractions. When properly pursued, they are necessary ingredients in the achievement of the good life.

Josef Pieper, in his cult classic *Leisure: The Basis of Culture*, argues that leisure is a necessary condition for both individual and communal survival, growth, and progress. Pieper claims that because so many of us are addicted, by choice or circumstances, to the idolatry of work, we are not sure what leisure is and—even worse—in the words of Bertrand Russell we have been tricked into accepting a life without leisure as normal.[24]

Strictly speaking, for Pieper, leisure is not simply a form of recreation or diversion, nor is it the natural result of rest, relaxation, or amusement. Although it is necessary to be free of the toil and moil of the everyday burdens of work for it to occur, leisure is primarily a mental set, a psychological orientation, a condition of one's soul or spirit. For him, leisure is an attitude of non-activity, of not being busy, of inner calm, a commitment to silence, meditation, observation, and letting things be. Leisure is a way of life and not just the inevitable byproduct of holidays, spare time, weekends, or a vacation:

> *Leisure is a form of silence, of that silence which is the prerequisite of the apprehension of reality.... For leisure is a receptive attitude of the mind, a contemplative attitude....*

> *Leisure, like contemplation, is of a higher order than the* vita activa *[active life].... It is only in and through leisure that the "gate of freedom" is opened and man can escape from the closed circle of that "latent dread and anxiety"...[which is] the mark of the world of work.*[25]

To be leisurely, says Pieper, is a choice. To be leisurely is to be disengaged from the tedium of tasks—to be open, observant, and receptive to issues outside of self and one's immediate needs. Leisure is time given to contemplation, wonder, awe, and the development of ideas. Leisure is about creativity, insight, unregulated thoughts. It is about intellectual activity, not intellectual work or utilitarian problem solving. It is about desire, wonder, and unbridled curiosity. For Thomas Aquinas, leisure is the vehicle, the necessary condition for the *vita contemplativa* (life of the mind), which is the "noblest mode of human life" and the primary means by which we transcend the limits of the human condition.[26]

Like Aristotle before him, Pieper believed that leisure is the catalyst for culture and the development of philosophy, theology, poetry, and the arts. Culture is all that is beyond the immediate sphere of wants and needs—things not absolutely necessary, useful, or utilitarian, but what ultimately defines us as a species or a group.

Epilogue

We do not believe in ourselves
until someone reveals
that deep inside us
something is
valuable,
worth listening to,
worthy of our trust,
sacred to our touch.
Once we believe in ourselves
we can risk
curiosity,
wonder,
spontaneous delight
or any experience that reveals the human spirit.

e.e. cummings

I have been a student and teacher of philosophy my entire adult life. I have no regrets whatsoever that I did not listen to my father about going to law school, or going to medical school, or—horror of horrors—working for him in the family business. If I could live my life over again, I would make the same choice I did then. (Except, of course, I would definitely have kept that Microsoft stock I sold in the mid-eighties.) Philosophy, for me, has been a way of life. A way of negotiating the mysteries and wonders of existence. A way of looking at the world. A way of thinking about the unthinkable and the unbearable.

Over the years, I've basically remained a dilettante in my approach to philosophy. I keep jumping from topic to topic as my interest and curiosity move me. Although I've eclectically pursued the discipline, I've done so passionately, and I've continuously struggled, in the words of Augustine of Hippo, to be "a thoughtful person in the world." In looking back on my research and writings, the single most important personal lesson I've learned is a very basic one, yet one many try very hard to deny or avoid: *We humans are communal creatures. Life is primarily a collective enterprise, not a solitary one. We are dependent on each other to survive and thrive. Our collective existence requires us to continually make choices about what we ought to do in regard to others.*

English philosopher and novelist Iris Murdock argues that to respond to the world objectively, you first have to perceive it clearly and dispassionately. This, says Murdock, requires a kind of "unselfing." She argues that "anything which alters consciousness in the direction of unselfishness, objectivity, and realism is to be connected with virtue…. [And] virtue is the attempt to pierce the veil of selfish consciousness and gain the world as it really is."[1] The simple fact is that the world is not just about "me, myself, and I." It is always about "me and others." Neither happiness nor wisdom are possible without the ability to step outside of the protective cocoon of self and be empathetic, sympathetic, and understanding of the wants, needs, and desires of others. In the words of legendary and philosophically-minded college basketball coach John Wooden, "Happiness begins were selfishness ends."

Absorption-in-self is not a new phenomenon. Its footprint and pathology are well-documented in our history as a species. From the ranks of the proletariat to the members of the princely caste, we can find innumerable examples of our collective inability and unwillingness to be empathetic, sympathetic, or understanding of the wants, needs, and desires of others. Ernest Becker has argued that we recapitulate the tragedy of Narcissus by living too much of our lives absorbed with self. "As Aristotle somewhere put it," says Becker, "luck is when the guy next to you gets hit with an arrow. Twenty-five hundred years of history have not changed man's basic narcissism; most of the time, for most of us, this is still a workable definition of luck." If we care about anyone else at all, said Becker, it is only after we have first taken care of ourselves.[2] To be parochial but not necessarily unpatriotic, I believe that too many of us in the United States are convinced that the pursuit of happiness is primarily a solitary, not a communal, experience.

Even though there is no exact science to happiness, and no set of absolute principles to study, its illusory nature does not deter us. We believe that happiness, whatever it is, is the *summum bonum* ("the ultimate good") of life. Psychologist David G. Myers, who has studied happiness (AKA "life satisfaction") for more than thirty years, points out a number of paradoxes regarding its pursuit and achievement. Too many of us, says Myers, believe that happiness is primarily about *things* and *self-centered* behavior. The prevalent attitude is, "If I only had (more money, a new car, a bigger house, more clothes, a more prestigious job), I'd be happy." Or, "I can't be happy because of (poverty, ill health, bad luck, poor schooling)." Myers argues that the pursuit and achievement of happiness is not a singular, solitary, and self-centered activity. Happiness, he says, always occurs in the context of others and very often with the cooperation of others. Happiness is not a zero-sum game (one that says that if *I* achieve happiness, *you* cannot be happy, and vice versa). Happiness, like laughter, is primarily a collective, communal event, yet too many of us pursue happiness as if we were in competition with others and as if happiness were in limited supply. Because of this sense of competitiveness and scarcity, we focus on self, disregarding others and playing the game of life only to win—regardless of the consequences. Folk wisdom tells us, says Myers, that in the competition for happiness, what matters is success, not ethical sensitivity.[3]

I think that John Dewey was right: We have made a fetish out of the cult of "rugged individualism" and the "pursuit of happiness."[4] We think that all of our rights are personal, private, and proprietary, when in fact private rights always and only exist within the context of the collective community. Each generation needs to learn to forget itself on purpose, to let go of its ego needs, to step back from center stage, and at the very least be open to the voices and the needs of others. Simple prudence (to govern and discipline ourselves by the care of reason) should make us aware that we are not the only ones at the table, that issues and needs beyond our own must be addressed. Thomas Merton has argued that the paradox of both faith and ethics is the need to lose ourselves (in others) in order to find ourselves.[5]

In the end, I am convinced that the quality of our lives in regard to simple civility, the structure of politics, and the basic tenets of civilization itself are dependent on our ability to stand outside the shadow of self and make ethical choices about how we behave and interact with others. Without some common agreement regarding human rights and responsibilities, Thomas Hobbes' chilling prognostication in the *Leviathan* will be proven true: Life will be "solitary, poore, nasty, brutish, and short." For the catholic philosopher, this conclusion is just too small and unacceptable.

Mr. Spock, of Star Trek fame, always used the same Vulcan phrase when saying goodbye, "Live long and prosper!" Given everything I've said in this book, in saying goodbye to you the reader, allow me to slightly modify Spock's words. Remember, in order to live long and achieve wisdom and a modicum of prosperity, what is required is an appropriate balance of work, leisure, laughter, and love—as well as a steadfast belief in something far greater than just ourselves.

ENDNOTES

PROLOGUE

[1] John Stuart Mill, *On Liberty* (Longmans, Green, Reader, & Dryer, 1863), 68.

[2] James Rachels, *The Elements of Moral Philosophy* (New York: Random House, 1986, vi.

I. HOW I FELL IN LOVE WITH PHILOSOPHY

[1] Paul Strathern, *Socrates in 90 Minutes* (Chicago: Ivan R. Dee, 1997), 19.

[2] Christopher Phillips, *Socrates Café* (New York: W.W. Norton, 2001), 2, 3.

[3] Plato, *The Apology*, in *The Collected Dialogues of Plato*, edited by Edith Hamilton and Huntington Cairns (New York: Pantheon Books, 1961), 16-23.

[4] Vlastos quoted in Phillips, *Socrates Café*, 19.

[5] Ibid., 18-24.

[6] Plato, *Apology*, 15,16.

II. THE EXAMINED LIFE

[1] Ambrose Bierce, *Phantoms of a Blood-Stained Period: The Complete Civil War Writings of Ambrose Bierce* (University of Massachusetts Press, 2002), 144.

[2] William James, *William James: The Essential Writings* (SUNY Press, 1984), 2.

[3] Robert R. Provine, *Laughter* (New York: Viking, 2000), 11, 16.

[4] Sören Kierkegaard, *Repetition: An Essay in Experimental Psychology* (Princeton University Press, 1941)

[5] Blaise Pascal, *Thoughts: Letters, Minor Works* (P.F. Collier & Son, 1910), 78.

[6] Donald Barnhouse, *Realities Magazine* (Realities New York, 1980), January-February, 1980, 88.

[7] Horace M. Kallon, ed., *The Philosophy of William James*, (New York: The Modern Library, N.d.), 59.

[8] Jim Forest, "Biography of Dorothy Day," http://www.catholicworker.com/ddaybio.htm (accessed November 4, 2009).

[9] Gregory Bram, *The Priority of Labor* (Ramsey, N.J.: Paulist Press, 1982), 10.

III. THE NEED FOR MEANING

[1] Viktor Frankl, *Man's Search for Meaning* (New York, Pocket Books, 1963), 29.

[2] Ibid., 22.

[3] Ibid., 25.

[4] Ibid., 27.

[5] Ibid., 205.

[6] Ibid., 104.

[7] Ibid., 105.

[8] Ibid., preface xi.

[9] Ibid., 106.

[10] Ibid., 212-213.

[11] Ibid., 87-88.

IV. TOO MANY CHANGES, TOO MANY CHOICES

[1] Barry Schwartz, *The Paradox of Choice: Why More is Less* (New York: Ecco, 2004), 1.

[2] Ibid., 2.

[3] Ibid., 21.

[4] Ibid., 52-55.

[5] John De Graff, David Wann, and Thomas H. Naylor, *Affluenza* (San Francisco: Berrett-Koehler, 2001), 153.

[6] Matthew Fox, *The Reinvention of Work* (San Francisco: Harper, 1994), 7, 8.

[7] Barry Schwartz, *The Paradox of Choice*, 4.

V. THE SEVEN DEADLY SINS

[1] Gary Pence, "Sin: An Abusive Doctrine?", *Dialog*, 38:4, Fall 1999, 294.

[2] Henry Fairlie, *The Seven Deadly Sins Today* (Notre Dame: Nortre Dame Press, 1979), 21.

[3] Thomas B. Strong, *Christian Ethics* (London: Longmans, Green, and Co., 1986), 262

[4] John Bradshaw, *Reclaiming Virtue: How to Develop the Moral Intelligence to Do the Right Thing at the Right Time for the Right Reason* (New York: Bantam Books, 2009)

[5] Robert C. Solomon, editor, *Wicket Pleasures* (New York: Rowan and Littlefield, 1999), 2.

[6] Ibid., 3.

[7] Ibid.

[8] Thomas Aquinas, *Summa Theologia* I-II, Q. 84, Articles, 2,3,4 (New York: Benzinga Brothers, Inc., 1947), 962-965.

[9] George Otis Jr., *The God They Never Knew: The Tragedy of Religion Without Relationship*, http://biblical-theology.com/sin/otis3.htm, 03/28/05, 2.

[10] Ibid., 3.

[11] Craig Brown, "Out with the Deadly Sins, In with the New," *Scotsman* (Edinburgh), Feb. 7, 2005.

[12] Nancy Gibbs, "The New Road to Hell," *Time Magazine*, March 24, 2008, 78.

[13] Solomon Schimmel, *The Seven Deadly Sins* (New York: Oxford University Press, 1997), 4

[14] Gary Pence, "Sin: An Abusive Doctrine?", *Dialog*, 38:4, Fall 1999, 295.

[15] Robert C. Solomon, *Wicked Pleasures*, 10, 11.

[16] Ibid., 3.

[17] Elda Rotor, *Editors Note* in the Series, *The Seven Deadly Sins*, Oxford University Press, 2006 to 2006.

[18] Henry Fairlie, *The Seven Deadly Sins Today*, 13.

VI. A SHORT PRIMER ON MORAL COURAGE

[1] Ernest Becker, The Denial of Death (New York: Free Press, 1997), 36, 27.

[2] Ibid., xvii.

[3] Ibid., 11, 12.

[4] Ibid., 57

[5] Rushworth Kidder, Moral Courage (New York: Harper Collins, 2005), 7.

[6] Richard Strengel, "Mandela: His 8 Lessons of Leadership" Time Magazine, July 9, 2008.

[7] John Hendry, Between Enterprise and Ethics (New York: Oxford University Press, 2004)

[8] Brian J. Mahan, Forgetting Ourselves on Purpose (San Francisco: Jossey-Bass), 2002.

[9] Harold Kaplan, Benjamin Sadock, and Jack Grebb, Synopsis of Psychiatry, 7th ed. (Baltimore: William and Wilkins, 1994), 742-743.

[10] Patricia H. Werhane, "Moral Imagination and the Search for Ethical Decision Making and Management," *Business Ethics Quarterly*, Ruffin Series, 1 (n.d.): 81, 82.

[11] Ibid.

[12] Ibid., 88-91

[13] Jeff Pearlman, "'64 Murder Lives in Heart of Woman's Friend," *Chicago Tribune*, section I, 14, March 12, 2004.

VII. THE PHILOSOPHY OF WORK

[1] Howard Schwartz, *Narcissistic Project and Corporate Decay* (New York: New York University Press, 1990)

[2] Howard Schwartz, "Narcissistic Project and Corporate Decay: The Case of General Motors," *Business Ethics Quarterly*, 1 (3), 250.

[3] Robert Jackall, *Moral Mazes* (New York: Oxford Press, 1989), 11.

[4] Ibid., 70.

[5] Ibid., 6.

[6] Katherine McCourt, "College Students in a Changing Society," *The Heartland Conference*, May 1994, Loyola University Chicago, 5-22

[7] Jeffery K. Salkin, *Being God's Partner* (Woodstock, VT: Jewish Lights Press, 1994), 156.

[8] Everett C. Hughes, "Work and the Self," in John H. Rohrer and Muzafer Sherif, eds., *Social Psychology at the Crossroads* (New York: Harper, 1951), 313-23.

[9] Gregory Baum, *The Priority of Labor* (New York: Paulist Press, 1982), 10.

[10] Pope John Paul II, "Laborem Exercens," in *Gregory Baum, The Priority of Labor* (New York: Paulist Press, 1982), 104-6, 112.

[11] David M. Byers, ed., *Justice in the Marketplace: A Collection of Vatican and the U.S. Catholic Bishops and Economic Policy, 1891-1984*. Washington D.C.: United States Catholic Conference, 1985. Leo XIII. *Rerum Novarum*. Byers. 27.

[12] John Paul II 4.

[13] David Hollenbach, "Human Work and the Story of Creation: Theology and Ethics in *Laborem Exercens*." Houck and Williams. 63.

[14] Genesis 1:26-28.

[15] John Paul II 9.

[16] John Paul II 16.

[17] John Paul II 11.

[18] John Paul II 18

[19] Paul IV. *Populorum Progressio*. Byers. 22.

[20] Harry Braverman, *Labor and Monopoly Capital*, (New York: Monthly Review, 1974) 45.

[21] Gregory Baum, *The Priority of Labor*, (New York: Paulist Press, 1983) 9.

[22] John Paul II. *Laborem Exercens*. Byers. 6.

[23] John Paul II 26.

[24] John Paul II 22, 5.

[25] John Paul II 13.

[26] John Paul II 6.

[27] John Paul II 14.

[28] John Paul II 12-13.

[29] Leo XIII. *Rerum Novarum*. Byers. 51.

[30] Leo XIII 28.

[31] John Paul II 13.

[32] John Paul II 12.

[33] John Paul II 9.

[34] J.C. Raines, and D.C. Day-Lower, *Modern Work and Human Meaning*, (Philadelphia: Westminster, 1986) 15.

[35] John Paul II 1.

[36] Pius XI, *Quadragesimo Anno*, 61.

VIII. THE PHILOSOPHY OF LAUGHTER AND LEISURE

[1] Jim Holt, "Punch Line," *The New Yorker* (April 19 and 26, 2004): 184-190.

[2] Joshua W. Shenk, *Lincoln's Melancholy* (New York: Mariner Books, 2006), 181.

[3] Robert R. Provine, *Laughter: a scientific investigation* (New York: Penguin Group, 2000), 1-21.

[4] Ted Cohen, *Jokes: Philosophical Thoughts on Joking Matters* (Chicago: University of Chicago Press, 1999), ix.

[5] Bob Losyk, *Get a Grip: Overcoming Stress and Thriving in the Workplace* (John Wiley and Sons, 2005), 122.

[6] Ted Cohen, *Jokes: Philosophical Thoughts on Joking Matters* (Chicago: University of Chicago Press, 1999), 45.

[7] Eugene Fink, *Nietzche's Philosophy* (Continuum International Publishing Group, 2003), 157.

[8] André Comte-Sponville, *A Small Treatise on the Great Virtues* (New York: Metropolitan/Owl Books, 2001), 212.

[9] Ibid., 217.

[10] Ibid., 212

[11] Christopher Middleton, *Selected Letters of Frederick Nietzsche* (Hackett Publishing, 1996), 278.

[12] André Comte-Sponville, *A Small Treatise on the Great Virtues* (New York: Metropolitan/Owl Books, 2001), 221.

[13] See Thomas Cathcart and Daniel Klein, *Plato and Platypus Walk into a Bar* (New York: Abrams Image, 2007), 106 and 107.

[14] Diane Ackerman, *Deep Play* (New York: Random House, 1999), 6.

[15] Donald Hall, *LifeWork* (Boston: Beacon Press, 1993), 23.

[16] Erich Fromm, *The Sane Society* (Greenwich, Conn: Fawcett Publications, 1955), 253.

[17] Mark Harris, "The Name of the Game," *Utne Reader*, March-April 2001, 61 62.

[18] Robin Marantz Henig, "Taking Play Seriously," *The New Yorker Magazine*, February 17, 2008, 40.

[19] Al Gini, *The Importance of Being Lazy* (New York: Routledge, 2003), 113.

[20] William Manchester, *American Caesar: Douglas MacArthur 1880-1964* (Little, Brown, and Company, 1978).

[21] John Updike, "Farrell's Caddie," *The New Yorker*, February 25, 1991, 33.

[22] Timothy J. Carroll, "Reading About The Green," *Wall Street Journal*, March 22-23, 2008. W9.

[23] Wayne E. Oates, *Workaholics, Make Laziness Work For You* (Garden City, N.Y.: Doubleday and Co., 1978), 48, 49.

[24] Witold Rybczynski, *Waiting For the Weekend* (New York: Viking, 1991), 226.

[25] Josef Pieper, Leisure: *The Basics of Culture* (New York: New American Library, 1963), 40-44.

[26] Ibid., 27.

EPILOGUE

1. Iris Murdock, *The Sovereignty of Good* (London: Routledge Classics, 2001), 82, 91.

2. Ernest Becker, *The Denial of Death* (New York: Free Press Paperbacks, 1997), 2,3.

3. David G. Myers, *The Pursuit of Happiness* (New York: William Morrow and Company, 1952).

4. John Dewey, *Individualism Old and New* (New York: Capricorn, 1962).

5. A.E. Carr, *A Search for Wisdom and Spirit: Thomas Merton's Theology of Self* (Norte Dame, IN: University of Norte Dame Press, 1988), 26.

INDEX OF NAMES

ACKNOWLEDGMENTS

If we should deal out justice only,
in this world,
who would escape?
No, it is better to be generous,
and in the end more profitable,
for it gains gratitude for us,
and love.

Mark Twain

The original idea for this book was planted in my brain by my erstwhile agent, Danielle Egan-Miller. But the only reason this book is seeing the light of day is Greg Pierce, the publisher of ACTA Publications. Five minutes into my sales pitch, Greg asked me to stop. I, of course, assumed the worst. He looked at me and said, "Fine, I like it, let's do it." Greg has been both a tough critic and a loyal fan for twenty years, and I'm thankful for both aspects of our relationship.

Finally, this book wouldn't physically exist except for the careful and committed work of Sondra Heine and her two assistants, Jennifer Palarz and Ashley Diltz, and the design artistry of Patricia Lynch and Tom Wright. Charles Fiore did a careful editing job, although all errors remain mine or God's or both.

Thanks to all!